Personalities

Personalities

A Selection from the Writings

of

A. A. Baumann

Essay Index Reprint Series

Originally published by:
Macmillan & Co. Ltd.

BOOKS FOR LIBRARIES PRESS
FREEPORT, NEW YORK

First Published 1936
Reprinted 1968

This selection from A. A. B.'s writings is
dedicated to his lifelong friend Browning,
in accordance with what the Editor believes
would have been the Author's wish.

LIBRARY OF CONGRESS CATALOG CARD NUMBER:

68-54323

MANUFACTURED
BY
HALLMARK LITHOGRAPHERS, INC.
IN THE U.S.A.

FOREWORD

I HAVE chosen from the work of Arthur Anthony
Baumann what I think gives the essence of that
remarkable critic of men, life and politics. I had
hoped, at first, to arrange the articles and essays in
some organic order corresponding to the growth
and development of A. A. B.'s opinions and personality. This I found impossible because so much
of his best work, like some of Macaulay's best, was
inspired by the contemplation of some book sent
for review. There was naturally a kinship in the
type of book. Nobody, for example, would have
invited A. A. B. to deliver himself on a House-
wife's Miscellany. Nevertheless, the disconnected
nature of the stimulus made such a scheme
impracticable.

Nor was this my only difficulty. A. A. B.,
though in the *Saturday Review, Truth* and the
Evening Standard he has unnumbered, though alas!
too often anonymous columns to his credit, permitted himself book publication only on three
occasions. He was in his choice of what he col-
lected unduly severe with himself. He reprinted
of set purpose what was most objective. He never

conceived that his public might have been as interested in A. A. B. as in his subjects. He did not conceive this because—strange and refreshing man—he was himself more interested in the subjects than in A. A. B. This was perhaps a common virtue in the reign of Victoria. It has become so rare among us that we can hardly believe a man to have written about Napoleon until he has described in detail his whippings at school and the wart on the forehead of the woman who kept the tuck-shop.

A. A. B.'s method, which is the classic method, needs no defence. It does, however, further intensify the difficulty of showing by arrangement the expansion in the author's spirit. He is thinking, you see, rather of the expansion or contraction of England, and his attitude to that is unchanged from first to last. His politics may be right or wrong, that does not at this point matter much. What does matter here is that they had a sole and unswerving purpose and care—the love of his country, as he saw it, when he entered the Parliament of Disraeli as a young man. Like Disraeli in his methods, he was a romantic realist—one of those who impose the great shape of imagination upon facts and change them. It was not given to

A. A. B., as it was to Disraeli, to crown the theories of youth with the triumphant action of his later years. A. A. B., therefore, lived with his first generous impulses and not they but the world altered, so that in the end the young reformer—for such he was—holding to the same end and nursing the same beliefs, is pointed at by time as a reactionary. It is, of course, a name that might equally, and for the same reason, have been accorded to Mr. Standfast in the *Pilgrim's Progress*.

I find, I need hardly say, nothing ignoble in so long-unchanged a devotion to one faith, and I will not, in its presence, be guilty of an unworthy sneer by commenting on its rarity to-day. Single-hearted faith has always and at all times been rare. But, as it is rare, it has its literary difficulties. Its very consistency denies it something of the sparkle that is generated by the friction of rapid transitions from one side of the House of Commons to the other. Such politicians have the advantage over A. A. B. They are lighted with the brilliance of their own tergiversations. In the quieter path that A. A. B. has chosen to tread, his single and calm outlook shows tranquil beside the exploits of adventurous jack-o'-lanthorns.

Obedient, therefore, to what I believe he would have preferred, I have begun the selection with a wise and measured disquisition on "The Victorian Tradition", and ended it with a life's confession of faith, pursued to the end, in the eloquent preface to Burke's *Letter to a Noble Lord*. For A. A. B. the great torch, held aloft by Burke, was carried to the edge of darkness by the last of the Victorians, and so out! It is appropriate, therefore, that the book should begin with the last survivor, as it were grinding out the embers with his heel, and end with the light, which in A. A. B.'s view never again will be on land or sea.

I have followed the introductory essay with three papers, which I have listed under "Private Personalities". I have placed these in the forefront because they are the nearest approach to anything like self-portraiture in A. A. B.'s work. Even here the portrait is almost entirely one drawn by inference. The author is determined to preserve his spiritual anonymity. He will not in the amiable contemporary mode undress in public; he will not even appear in carpet slippers. He is the voice of the oracle, which does not dissipate its authority by appearing in a bowler hat immediately that the performance is finished.

As far, however, as he would permit self-revelation, these three papers do give some hint of the young man whose portrait I have so often seen in the group-photograph of Balliol, Hergoevilla Club, 1878, which hangs at No. 44 Hyde Park Square. The face of the young man has achieved the miracle of squaring the circle. It is perfectly chubby, and at the same time square-jawed in a quite alarming manner for one so young. The mixture of steady determination allied to affection for life and a very few chosen spirits, is there plain for anyone to see. I have pictured that forcible youth rising in his place in the Union to denounce Mr. Gladstone's Bulgarian atrocities campaign. The square-jawed element was out for murder, the round-cheeked for the enjoyment of the rolling phrase. The two entities coalesced, and the result was one of the most memorable speeches ever delivered at the Union by an Undergraduate.

I have printed next after these partially private reminiscences a wide selection of "Political Personalities", and these I have grouped alphabetically, as there was little to be gained by any other arrangement. These papers have, apart from their general political significance, a fresh and

living interest. In every case—even in the case of
men long dead—A. A. B. writes of these great
names as their contemporary—and not as a mere
contemporary gossip-writer. With all of them,
from Mr. Balfour at the head of the list to Lord
Salisbury at the end, he had regular dealings in
the political sphere. It is therefore possible for
him, writing in the second or third decade of the
twentieth century, to comment in the present
tense on persons of the 'eighties. This in any case
produces an odd feeling of excitement in the
reader. But when the commentator not only has a
long memory, but as with A. A. B. a sharp, clear
vision for incident and a felicitous pen, we are
faced with an almost unique performance in
literary biography. Such a small incident, for
example, as Mr. Speaker Peel's indignation with
A. A. B. because of a fancied slight, has the freshness of last night's storm in a tea-cup, and throws
us back with a turn of the wrist out of the reign
of George into the lobbies of good Queen Victoria's
day.

The variety of the persons in the list enables
A. A. B. to cover every aspect of politics as he
saw them. With Fowler and Gorst he gives us his
picture of the Third Party—not, it seems, so much

a Third Party as an individual star-turn. In Lord Goschen he finds an opportunity of discussing the business man in politics, and incidentally reveals his charming reverence for anybody who understands, or purports to understand, the mysteries of Foreign Exchange. In Lord Randolph Churchill and Lord Curzon—two how differently gifted figures, and yet alike in the ultimate disappointment of their ultimate ambition—he indicates with trenchant simplicity the glories and miseries of the politician's life. Labouchere is a study of the Man who Knew too Much—a character later expanded into a commentary upon civilisation by G. K. Chesterton. While Mr. Balfour and Lord Salisbury are the culmination of the great Cecil family with their grace, their vigour, and as the result of centuries of tradition, with their broad, undeviating statesmanship.

A student of the real meaning of Victorian politics—if such a one survives—will learn more from these first-hand portraits, however he may dislike the opinions that accompany them, than from twenty guesses of later historians. An ounce of fact, if it is accurately weighed, is still worth a ton of theory. But as to theory, A. A. B. expresses himself in one or two literary excursions which I have inserted after the politicians, under the title "Literary Personalities". A. A. B. is not at all a literary critic in the ordinary sense. He goes for the man rather than for the matter. This is his method also in politics, and, as in politics, so in literature the result is surprisingly satisfactory. Nobody will rise from reading the paper on "Lord Chesterfield", for example, with a better appreciation of that nobleman's capacity as a writer. But a person who has not so much a literary taste as an appetite for life, will observe with a shock that he has been taught something about manners—an unusual experience with a contemporary critic. And when such a one has perused the dissertation on Frank Harris, he will probably be glad that he personally was not an acquaintance of A. A. B.'s who fell under his displeasure.

In conclusion I have printed before the preface to *A Letter to a Noble Lord*, two general articles on the Victorian spirit, "Queen Victoria's Middle Years" and "Disraeli's Meridian", under the title "Political Impersonalities". These are probably the two best articles that A. A. B. ever wrote, and, as a Tory's picture of the irretrievable and beloved past, would be hard to beat in any political writing anywhere. The account of Disraeli, in particular, is memorable because it is the only common-sense estimate of that startling character which I know. To most biographers he is a character in a melodrama, a film or a fairy-story. They write of him with pens dipped either in hyssop or alternatively in rose-water. A. A. B. has used ink.

Well, there it is—and now let the book speak for itself, as it will and must if it attracts a tithe of the attention which it deserves. For my part, to have done this little to redirect public attention to a considerable name is not so much a labour of love as a happy excursion. To have known A. A. B. has for me been, I will not say a liberal, because that would be a paradox, it has been a conservative education. I have seen the steadiness of outlook in public affairs brought to govern and control private discomfort with patience, dignity and strength. Through long and aching years of illness A. A. B. remained unshaken and unshakable in his allegiance to the ideas that had guided his political life. "Here I am and here I stay", he said with a grim smile to paralysis, a cruel and creeping invader. With his tidy air of a smaller and more spiritual Mr. Pickwick, he twinkled at his rapacious and yet defeated enemy through his glasses, "Where is your sting?" Where indeed and where his victory, since the written word outlasts the crawling enmities of time and death.

HUMBERT WOLFE

CONTENTS

PERSONALITIES

Political Impersonalities

I

THE VICTORIAN TRADITION

I

THE VICTORIAN TRADITION

CENTURIES are, we know, artificial divisions of time, and I have not discovered by whom or for what purpose that method of chronology was first adopted. It does, however, seem that at the end of a period, roughly approximating to a hundred years, a new generation, with new habits and modes of speech, insensibly emerges into existence. Modern historians, like Green and Trevelyan, are apt to sneer at the idea that the births and deaths of kings and queens have anything to do with the destiny of mankind. Those who, like myself, believe in personal rather than tendencious records, and agree with Disraeli that biography is the best history, will find their theory confirmed by the fact that for the last four centuries, at least, changes of tradition have been synchronous with the deaths of British Sovereigns. It must be so generally, because when a powerful monarch dies, there pass with him or her a group of courtiers, who set the fashion, and a group of ministers, who govern the State. The death of

Elizabeth ended the Tudor tradition. The Stuart tradition lasted, with the interruption of the Cromwellian decade, until the death of Anne in 1714. The Hanoverian tradition lasted until after Waterloo, and the death of George III in 1820. The painful interregnum filled by the sons of George III was closed by the accession of Victoria in 1837. At the end of the last century, between 1898 and 1903, there died Mr. Gladstone, Queen Victoria and Lord Salisbury, and with them was interred the Victorian tradition. Not of course sharply or immediately, for some of the great Queen's servants, Morley, Harcourt and Bannerman, survived her, and two, Lords Oxford and Grey, lived till after the Great War. King Edward, with his unerring instinct, felt that some relaxation of Court etiquette was necessary, but he did his best, though unsuccessfully, to maintain the Victorian tradition in politics. That, however, was not possible after Lord Salisbury's death. The distraction, or more plainly the destruction, of the Unionist party in the hands of Messrs. Arthur Balfour and Joseph Chamberlain led to the polls of 1905, and after that the Victorian tradition perished utterly.

I am a Victorian Tory, naked and unashamed.

I make no pretence to impartiality, or attempt to defend my prejudices. I do but touch the Great War in connection with Lords Oxford and Grey. Enough has been written on that subject by greater pens than mine. Armageddon apart, everything done after 1906 is for me a step on the easy slope that leads unlimited democracy to its nadir of helplessness and corruption.

The Trades Disputes Act contradicts the principles of personal freedom and equality before the law, and places our industrial system at the mercy of the trade unions. The Finance Act of 1910, and the unfair incidence of war taxation, have led to the break-up of landed estates and the ruin of the territorial aristocracy. The Parliament Act has placed us under single-chamber government. The Reform Act of 1918, that crowning exhibition of sentiment and recklessness, rushed through Parliament without debate in the last year of the war, added twelve million voters to the register, including recipients of parish relief and the wives of existing voters. The surrender of five-sixths of Ireland to the party of murder and treason by Unionist statesmen completes the tale.

What do I mean by the Victorian tradition? During Victoria's reign the government of the country was conducted by men round whom the confidence of the country had gathered during many years of public service. Their characters and accomplishments were known to everyone, and they took their trust seriously and reverently. Burke said of Admiral Keppel, "There was something high about him". There was something high about statesmen like Goschen, Harcourt, Beach, Salisbury, Hartington, Balfour, Morley, who governed England during the last twenty years of the last century. To the early Victorian period, between 1840 and 1880, belong Macaulay, Peel, Cobden, Bright, Palmerston, Gladstone, Disraeli, Lowe, Derby, surely a constellation of orators such as no country ever produced before. Nor was it only of eloquent leaders that this age was prolific; it was distinguished by the number of independent members of Parliament such as Molesworth, Burdett, Grote, Roebuck, Stuart Mill, Horsman, men of letters and free-spoken country gentlemen, who would have scorned to be told what they were to say, and how they were to vote.

I may be wrong in placing the Augustan age of parliamentary government in Victoria's reign. I like to remember Cromwell's adjuration to his petitioners to bethink them, in Christ's name, that they might be wrong. I will therefore call the corroborative testimony of, not another Tory, but of a Whig, "of purest ray serene". Sir Almeric Fitzroy, descendant of a Whig duke, was for thirty years Clerk of the Privy Council, and for that item lived very near the rose.

It is, of course, essential that the Clerk of the Privy Council should be a gentleman, because his relations with the Sovereign and the Lord President of the Council are intimate and confidential. He is a liaison officer between the ceremonial and executive parts of the Constitution; and though the size of the Council called Privy, which has some 250 members, has necessarily deprived it of power, there are always some dozen of its number who know everything that is to be known about Kings and Cabinets.

Sir Almeric betrays no confidences and makes no unkind personal observations. But the two closely packed volumes of his *Memoirs* [1] are in themselves a very serious indiscretion, none the less grave because it is doubtful whether the author has written for our amendment or our amusement.

[1] Sir Almeric Fitzroy, *Memoirs*. Hutchinson. 2 vols.

On almost every page Sir Almeric Fitzroy reveals the fact that, after the death of Lord Salisbury, the government of England was conducted with a levity, a personal rancour and an unscrupulousness that sometimes outrages decency and often staggers credibility. Such a revelation of carelessness and extravagance is dangerous knowledge.

Sir Almeric, with a personal admiration of Mr. Balfour and an earnest desire to be fair to Mr. Chamberlain, strains his courtly vocabulary to its limits to conceal his contempt for the weakness and sophistry of the Tory leader and his anger at the ruthless indiscipline of his Radical colleague. Mr. Balfour began as a Free Fooder, then announced that he had no settled convictions either way, and finally was driven into declaring that Tariff Reform was the first plank in the constructive platform of the Conservative Party.

Mr. Balfour paid a visit to Esher Place, and upon being asked by his hostess, Lady Helen Vincent (as she was then), whether he would take tea or coffee, replied that he didn't care which. "Oh! I see, you have no settled convictions on the point." The random shaft, drawn by a lovely hand, pierced the mail of the philosopher, and Sir

Almeric tells us that Mr. Balfour was visibly "nettled".

Great parties are not kept together by "the gossamer web" of Socratic subtlety, nor are they to be bludgeoned into following the flag of a political corsair. The odd thing is that when the outside world could see that the Tory Party was heading straight for destruction, Taper Hood, better known as the Pink 'Un, and Tadpole Hughes, the helpless agent at the Central Office, assured their chiefs and the Carlton Club that the Radicals couldn't even form a Government!

Such boastful incompetence met the punishment it deserved. Sir Henry Campbell-Bannerman formed, in December 1905, the strongest Government, as regards individual capacity, of modern times, and, by the folly of the Unionist leaders and the accident of war, one of the longest-lived. The new Prime Minister had been trained under Mr. Gladstone and Sir William Harcourt, and for two years the gravity and decorum of public life were kept up.

With the Premiership of Mr. Asquith the reign of laxity began. Then was the era of Christian names all round. From the hour when a famous financier addressed Mr. Balfour as "Arthur" in a club, and Tory and Radical leaders played bridge together, "the game of lor and order was up". The phrase which Bismarck applied to Salisbury, "a lath painted to look like iron", was far more applicable to Mr. Asquith. He could not, or would not, control the slap-dash methods of Messrs. Churchill and Lloyd George.

Side by side with the financial mess of the 1909 Budget proceeded the bargaining with Mr. John Redmond over Home Rule and the House of Lords. The 80 Irish Nationalists knew that as long as the House of Lords retained its constitutional powers no Home Rule Bill could pass. They also knew that their 80 votes could turn out the Government. Even when they had, by means which we shall never know for some years to come, tied the hands of the House of Lords, the Government found that they had forgotten Ulster, and began shilly-shallying, not knowing, like Macbeth, whether to go back or forward. General Seely, a Tory deserter, thought of the Army, but found the officers wouldn't march. Mr. Churchill, another Tory deserter, sent a wireless order to the Navy, which he almost immediately revoked. Never a word did anybody hear about the consequences to poor England and

Scotland. On this wretched scene of personal squabbling and parochial politics descended Armageddon. Even then personal rivalry and indecision continued. Lord Morley, discussing Cabinets with the Clerk of the Privy Council in 1912, said, "One hears this or that criticised on public grounds, when one knows that it is merely the expression of A's dislike of B".

The only member of the Government who worked seriously at his job, and to whose brains and courage the country owed the landing of the Expeditionary Force, was Lord Haldane. Yet he was discarded on the formation of the first Coalition in May 1915, owing to the jealousy of some of his colleagues, and the fear of the rabble who mobbed him and broke his windows. Revenge is a dish which is best eaten cold, and eight years later Lord Haldane was again on the Woolsack when Mr. Asquith was rejected by Paisley.

On the expulsion of the Lord Chancellor the Prime Minister surpassed himself in casualness. Being away from town, he sent a wireless message to the King submitting Lord Buckmaster's name for the Great Seal! Fancy Lord Beaconsfield or Mr. Gladstone sending a wireless message to

Queen Victoria that somebody should be appointed Lord Chancellor!

From 1916 to 1922 Mr. Lloyd George was dictator. Though in the summer of 1918 the Prime Minister knew that the duration of the war was an affair of months, and though he was repeatedly warned by the Home Office, the Board of Trade and the Ministry of Labour that the demobilisation of five million men would require the most elaborate preparations and precautions, nothing whatever was done to meet the emergency. It was only when threatening crowds began to march from the East End on the Ministry of Labour in Whitehall that the public money began to fly. Then it was discovered that nobody knew what to do except to bribe somebody to go away or to stay where he was.

On January 8, 1919, there is this entry in the Clerk of the Council's diary: "I learnt from Stamfordham through the telephone that all hope of a Council this week must be abandoned. He found a most chaotic condition prevailing at No. 10. I asked him whether with his knowledge of Downing Street, he was surprised, at which he laughed."

How can such a system produce great statesmen? I do not ignore the fact that since the break-up of the Coalition in 1922, there has been a great improvement in manners under Mr. Baldwin, at any rate in ministerial circles. The Government of England is no longer treated as a gamble or an exciting farce. But what the Government has gained in seriousness it seems to have lost in strength. Its striking power has gone; subordination has disappeared; the Government is unable to prevent an avowed Bolshevik from holding up the industry of the country for nine months. It is unable to say no to any demand on the public purse. These things suggest the interesting question whether, as we approach universal democracy, great statesmen will any longer be producible commodities.

Goldwin Smith, in his once-famous essay on Cromwell, observed that the importance of great men in history becomes less as civilisation goes on. "A Timon or an Attila towers unapproachably above his horde; but in the last great struggle which the world has seen the Cromwell was not a hero, but an intelligent and united nation." This is an allusion to Abraham Lincoln, for these essays were written in 1867. "And to whatever age they may belong, the greatest, the most god-like are men, not gods. They are the offspring, though the highest offspring, of their age."

If Cromwell escaped the intoxication of power, and bore himself as the trustee of God; if amidst the temptations of arbitrary rule, he preserved his reverence for law; it was because he was one of a religious and law-loving people. That great men are the creatures, not the creators of their age, put shortly, is the thesis of Goldwin Smith. If it was true in the seventeenth century, how much truer is it in the twentieth?

Pitt, the son of Chatham, is the last of Goldwin Smith's *Three English Statesmen*. William Pitt became Chancellor of the Exchequer and Leader of the House of Commons in 1783, at the age of twenty-three, and he was Prime Minister at the age of twenty-four. Surely, people used to say, here was a heaven-born, or a heaven-sent statesman; here was a miracle of genius! William Pitt was an extraordinarily clever youth; but if you consider that he was the son of the Earl of Chatham, who had died a few years before, in a sunset of glory, and if you recall the conditions of the political world at that time, there was nothing miraculous about it.

In order to realise the politics of that hour, you

need only imagine the Carlton and Reform Clubs, next to one another in Pall Mall, containing the entire political world, as disputing, dividing and settling the Government of England between the Committees of the two establishments, with a large Secret Service fund supplied partly by the dukes, partly by the Treasury and partly by Buckingham Palace. With that system, a boy Premier is no such wonder. But how completely Pitt was the creature of his age is proved by his abandonment of all the principles with which he entered public life and of the most important measures of his first Administration. Pitt began, as became his father's son, as a Whig and a student of Adam Smith. From the fact that Chatham's picture hangs in the hall of the Carlton Club, it is possible that its members think he was a Tory. The elder Pitt was an advanced Whig, and would have been horrified to hear of his son turning Tory. During his first four years the youthful Minister introduced a Reform Bill for abolishing by purchase the rotten boroughs, and for free trade with Ireland, and prepared himself for a stretch of peace and economy. By the close of the sixth year he was forced to become a Tory Imperialist. His surrender, however, was no sordid or squalid affair. He was not conquered by a caucus, by a cheap press or the "yea and nay of general ignorance". He bowed to Burke and the French Revolution.

It is necessary to distinguish between heroes and great men. To constitute heroism there must be action; no mere writer or speaker ever was a hero, for, as Byron asked, who that could act would write? Missolonghi, not *Don Juan*, made Byron a hero. The hero must also sacrifice himself, I think, unto death, for a cause from which he draws no material advantage.

Nelson, we are all agreed, was a hero; but how would it have been with him if he had lived to be made a duke, ageing on a large pension at Merton with Emma? Worse still, if he had become a politician? Marlborough survived Blenheim to be tried for peculation. Wellington outlived Waterloo by thirty-five years, to sink into a commonplace partisan.

Looking back at the Great War, I see only two heroes, and they were women. Edith Cavell knew well that in helping her countrymen to escape from the Germans she was, according to the laws of war, liable to be shot at dawn, and she was shot. Elsie Inglis, being a doctor, realised clearly that in fighting the typhus epidemic in Serbia she could not hope to save her own life. Her only reward was the knowledge that came to her before death that she had helped to save many Serbians. Well does Mr. David Masters say in *The Conquest of Disease*, a wonderful book, that "Dr. Elsie Inglis was a very gallant woman, and her fight with typhus is one of the most glorious pages in medical history". Mass production, with its resultant standardisation, is obviously against the production of great men. "In the bare and level plain of democracy every ant-heap is a mountain and every thistle is a forest tree." That was Robert Lowe's picturesque way of putting, in one of his speeches against the extension of the franchise in 1867, the fact that what is called equality, as produced by legislation, is a dreary, monotonous uniformity. A great man is, as has been said, the creature of his age, but a creature of exaggerated egotism, a magnifying mirror. The tendency of an age of multiplied competition and perverted values is to smother emergence, and to distract the applause or recognition of struggling greatness.

There are ten thousand novels published every year, I am told. How many Austens and Thackerays and Trollopes pass undetected in that crowd? Some of "the best sellers" I find it impossible to read, while often I come across a novel by an unknown, or third-rate (in the publisher's estimation), writer which is to my taste as good as the best of the last century.

Take politics, the noblest arena for the testing of brains and character. Is it not true that while there are some brilliant, eloquent, wise patriots in both Houses of Parliament, the best are not quite great men? Everybody respects, and many admire Mr. Baldwin. He is the kind of Minister who in the eighteenth century would have been referred to in the royal closet as "notre bon Baldwin". He may be classed with Addington and Liverpool; but surely not with Canning and Disraeli? Lord Birkenhead and Mr. Churchill excited the daily wonder of the spectators by their feats on the political trapeze: they "wear without co-rival" all the honours of the parliamentary field. But how many competent judges would dispute the assertion that they were not quite great men? Was not Lord Oxford the king of the Not-quites, with Mr. Lloyd George attendant as the great Might-have-been?

Take the greatest war of all time, when whole nations took the field in the place of small professional armies. There were five armies under the British command, each one as big as the army commanded at Waterloo by Wellington. Yet who can name a really great soldier, I mean of the Marlborough–Wellington–Bonaparte class, thrown up by this Armageddon? The battle of Jutland is the subject of angry dispute to this hour. But no one contends that it was a Trafalgar. Is there a Kemble, a Kean, a Siddons or an Irving on the stage? No; but the general level of acting is raised. Quite so; we live among the Not-quites and the Just-nots.

I know there have been brave men after as well as before Agamemnon; that you must stand far off if you want to see the height and shape of the mountain, and all that. But how are great men to be created by an age which pours millions into the pockets of face-contortionists and prize-fighters; which thinks a Rugby back a greater man than a Cabinet Minister or a Judge; which crams the streets from Charing Cross to the Ritz to catch a glimpse of Chaplin or Fairbanks; and which turns its back with cold contempt upon the rest, the artistic and intellectual remnant? So ends my catechism. What the new generation may have in store for the world I do not know. Progress, the men of philosophy and science tell us, is the advance from status to contract. For the last twenty years we have been retreating from contract to status. Is it too much to hope that, if we must retrogress, we may at least recover some of the civic virtue of the last century?

II

PORTRAIT OF
A COLLEGE FRIEND

II

PORTRAIT OF A COLLEGE FRIEND

ARMINE KENT and I went up to Balliol together, he from Harrow and I from Wellington. Instead of sliding into his school set, he joined four or five of us in forming a little cave of rebels against the arrogance of the Balliol intellectuals.

Kent had been *proxime accessit* for a scholarship, so that we were proud of his support. Reaction against priggism, however, is not a wholly safe or beneficent motive; and for the first two years at all events it must be said that our "Youth was full of foolish noise". But Armine Kent could not have been passed over by the most purblind don, for there was no mistaking his distinction of mind and manners, which attracted the least impressionable. He was very handsome, and his manners had a charm which it was as difficult to define as to resist. On reflection, I think that he won people by a kind of appealing simplicity of address, by the directness and refinement of his language, and by a shyness which made him often reticent, but never rude. He had his moods of murmuring like most poets; but his strong sense of humour almost invariably broke the spell of melancholy. His humour was certainly original, for there was nothing he enjoyed laughing at so much as himself. He loved being chaffed, and the mimicry by a friend of any of his little peculiarities never failed to provoke peals of his laughter. Even in those early college days, when the principles of most young men are "sketchy", Kent developed two strongly marked qualities which never left him, and which formed the most salient features of his strange character. One was his almost morbid detestation of personal gossip. I call this quality almost morbid because it is obvious that if personal gossip were taboo, conversation would be reduced to "Shakespeare and the musical glasses", and the ordinary dinner-party would become a palace of silence. But Kent was so loyal and enthusiastic a friend that he could not bear to hear the slightest depreciation of anyone who stood, or had ever stood, to him in that relation. He resolutely discouraged the dissection of absent friends, and if he could not change the conversation, he either showed his disgust by silence, or he took up the cudgels and was often provoked into defending the indefensible. If his sensitiveness in this respect was a little excessive, it was surely a noble trait, for I can say of him, as I can say of no one else whom I know, that I never heard him speak evil of a living soul.

His other characteristic was his incapacity of submission to any authority. Though he loved Johnson almost as much as I do (which is saying a great deal), he did not agree with the Doctor that subordination is the keynote of society. He never could be got to allow that outside the law, one human being had any right to control another. He even denied the right of anyone to inquire into the affairs of another. A steely glare of resentment was the only answer he ever vouchsafed to the conventional query, "Well, what are you doing now?" The college and university authorities he despised and defied. We went in for Classical Greats together, and some examiner had set as the subject for the English essay, "Sympathy". Kent took up his pen and wrote quickly, "Sympathy is human, but apathy is divine". Then folding up his paper and throwing it on the table, he left the room. It is needless to say that he was ploughed, and had to take his pass degree a year later from St. Edmund's Hall.

In 1881 Armine Kent came to live in London,

and began to write prose and verse for magazines and newspapers. Articles and verses appeared in the *Fortnightly Review*, the *National Review*, the *Cornhill Magazine*, the *St. James's Gazette* and in a weekly journal called the *Court and Society Review*, long since extinct. It is to the credit of the race of editors that they at once discerned Kent's distinction of style. Famous London editors are, as a rule, "swift of despatch" rather than "easy of access" to unknown writers. Their desks are too often the dumping-ground of hopeless but persevering amateurs. When, therefore, a young man of twenty-five, without introductions, or social influence, or a prize-winner's record, finds his first productions published by editors like Mr. John Morley, Mr. Frederick Greenwood and Mr. James Payn, his is an unusual success. Mr. Payn wrote, of some lines which appeared in the *Cornhill Magazine*, that they had "the true bird note". Mr. Greenwood printed some verses at once in the *St. James's Gazette*, and wrote a courteous letter. Mr. John Morley, perhaps the best judge of literature then living, gave the greatest encouragement. I have seen two or three letters from Mr. Morley, saying that he would be glad if Kent would write more, and suggesting that he should

26

write regularly. It was about this time that Armine used to talk to me about writing a history of Latin poetry, a task for which no one was better qualified, and which we used playfully to refer to as his *magnum opus*. Here, then, was the beginning, under encouraging auspices, of a literary career that would certainly have brought some money and much reputation. But it was not to be. Several causes co-operated against Kent's living a strenuous and regular life. In the first place, he was the slave of that verbal fastidiousness which is common to all scholars, and to all in whom the sense of language is abnormally developed. Had you offered him the salary of a judge, I do not think that Kent could have written regularly, or to order. The journeyman work of literature was for him impossible, and in letters, as in any other profession, a man must go through the mill in order to succeed. Kent would only write when he had "something to say", as he put it. That, of course, is fatal to worldly success. Another cause of failure was the possession of a dangerously comfortable income, derived from capital which was unfortunately not tied up, and which before his death was pretty well used up. A third obstacle to industry was the hospitality

27

of his many friends, who a little spoiled him. Social popularity is a two-edged weapon. In the hands of one man it is a sword with which he opens the world's oyster: in the hands of another, it is an instrument of suicide. So many friends were delighted to have Kent in their houses for months on end, that what more could he demand of life? Their coverts, their trout streams and their stables were at his disposal; what more could any man want or get? It is a question often asked by joyous thirty, but seldom answered till after forty, when it is discovered that amusement bores and only business amuses.

Too quickly the years flew by in this pleasant fashion, until the habit of regular work became impossible. I am very glad that four or five years before his death I was able to introduce Kent to the editor of the *Saturday Review*. I know that the very valuable work which he did for the *Review* gave him keen pleasure.

His English verse and prose are occasionally obnoxious to the charge of obscurity. This was due, not to a confusion of thought, for no one's outlook on life was clearer, but to a desire to escape the commonplace and the obvious in expression.

I will give but one instance of his defiance of the great ones of the earth. Some days after the escapade in the "Greats" school Jowett sent for him, and recommended that he should, without taking his name off the books, go down for a term, and have another try at a degree. A few days later Kent was strolling down the Broad with a pipe in his mouth, when he ran bang into Jowett. Even the serenity of the great Head was disturbed, and Jowett visibly started. He sent for Kent again the same evening, and pointed out kindly, but firmly, that it was impossible for him to keep his name upon the books of Balliol. Kent accordingly saw that at last he must obey, and he therefore became a member of St. Edmund College, a small but very ancient foundation, whose resurrection the present day has witnessed; and as a member of that college, hitherto unheard of, he took his Pass degree.

Kent died of pneumonia at the age of forty-seven in his rooms in Jermyn Street. The callous, bustling world did not know him; but the image of the poet, the scholar, the loyal friend, will remain engraven on the memory of a few, clear-cut and ineffaceable.

III

BENJAMIN JOWETT

III

BENJAMIN JOWETT

THESE sketches of men of light and leading in the last quarter of Queen Victoria's reign call for a glance at the great Oxford Head who moulded the early mind of so many of them. The Master of Balliol was the guide, philosopher and friend of Sir Robert Morier and Lord Lansdowne, of Lords Oxford, Milner and Curzon, and of a great many able editors, whose lot is to bear the cross of anonymity. Jowett's influence therefore was pervasive, and extended unperceived beyond the walls of that hideous building, a cross between a barrack, a workhouse and a modern convent, which covers nearly the whole of one side of the Broad, almost smothering graceful little Trinity.

When I went up in 1874 the intellectual primacy of Balliol was unquestioned and indisputable. It was in a class by itself. After it came four reading colleges of much distinction—Corpus, University, New College and St. John's. Christ Church, since the spacious times of Harry

Chaplin and Walter Long were past, was still mourning the abolition of gentlemen commoners with their yellow tassels, and withdrew in haughty seclusion from the common current of University life.

"The House" turned its back on the river, and absolutely ignored the Union. Cricket it did play and cards, but in the seclusion of Bullingdon.

In my day Christ Church was in its transition period, and was neither fowl, nor flesh, nor good red herring. It did not mix with and lead "the young barbarians all at play", like Brasenose and Magdalen; it had ceased to be high-born, and was not yet high or even mezzo-brow. All this is changed now, for I remember in last year's (1926) Eight Christ Church contributed nearly half the crew. But at the time of which I am speaking the Cardinal's hat on a blazer was seldom seen in the streets,—men wore blazers, not bags, and also cap and gown untorn in the High—and I can not remember anyone at the House in the 'seventies who did anything in life except Lord Newton. The eclipse of Cardinal Wolsey's glorious abbey, which ought always to be the first college in Oxford, was the work of Jowett, who had routed the stately Liddell in the fight for the sons of the great families.

Balliol had gutted the House, and the Master, with his squeaky voice and round face, and cold commemorative eye, had stolen the gilded youth from the Dean. Perhaps, too, the upper classes were beginning to realise—they have a wonderful gift of intelligent anticipation—that the world was changing for their sons, who might conceivably be called upon at some more or less distant date to compete with intellectuals, "not bred in our kennel", to repeat the coarse phrase which a Whig peer applied to Gladstone. The Russells, Leveson-Gowers, Charterises, Fitzmaurices, Wallops, Portals, who would automatically have proceeded, in the previous generation, from Eton to Christ Church, now matriculated at Balliol, and were told they must read for honours.

The test of a great speech is whether it produces a change in the position of the speaker, as mirrored in the opinion of those around him. In 1877 I made a speech at the Union against Gladstone's Bulgarian atrocities agitation which transformed me in a night from nobody to somebody in my college and the University. I was elected President of the Union without opposition at the beginning of the next term. Balliol dons and scholars, who had looked askance at the commoner in loud checks and an eyeglass, now hailed me with "nods and becks and wreathéd smiles". On Jowett the effect of the speech was magical.

The Master had sent me down the term before for some tipsy revel, with expressions of cold contempt. He now invited me to spend part of the next Long at his Malvern villa, an honour rarely extended to any but scholars and exhibitioners. That was Jowett. As a host nobody could have been more charming, though his sherry was rather fiery, not to be allayed by his piping assurance that it was Amontillado. Dear old man! He used to walk me round the Beacon, dropping into my ear maxims about life and comments on its actors. The result was cumulative and remembered long afterwards. Two of his sayings only remain familiar, but wise enough, repeated probably to scores of his young friends, "never disappoint people" and "never explain yourself". I can't say I have observed either.

Jowett was fond of saying that Boswell was a genius, and some of his friends and pupils interpreted this judgement into a half-conscious wish that he, too, had been lucky enough to find a patient worshipper always at his elbow to record his conversation. Dr. Evelyn Abbott and Dr. Lewis Campbell have done much, both by their previous *Life* and by the later volume of *Letters*, to give the world a nearer view of the greatest college Head of his day. But neither *Life* nor *Letters* can give any idea of Jowett's daily talk, which was quite as remarkable in its way as that of Dr. Johnson.

Jowett and Johnson had truly many striking points of difference, but they were superficial, or related to those habits which are the result of circumstances rather than an expression of character. Dr. Johnson was a slovenly Bohemian, idle, and often intemperate. Dr. Jowett detested Bohemianism and eccentricity of all kinds, was a model of neatness in his dress, and a pattern of precision in his hours. Johnson bawled and Jowett chirped; but the mental attitude of the two men towards the world and their fellow-creatures was the same. Both had the virtue, or the vice, of incredulity, and the Master of Balliol hesitated as little as the Sage of Fleet Street to give the lie direct to anyone whom he disbelieved.

The pendant to Johnson's "Sir, don't tell that story again: you can't think how poor a figure you make in telling it", was Jowett's favourite comment, "There's a great deal of hardy lying in the world, especially amongst people whose character it is impossible to suspect". Both moralists had a hearty contempt for the *cui bono* school of philosophy, and perhaps an exaggerated admiration for those who, in Johnson's words, are helping to drive on the system of the world. In the presence of both, intellectual pretension stood abashed, and loose talk was repressed. Both practised conversation not merely as an art but as a duty, and both influenced their generation a great deal more by their spoken than their written words.

We doubt, for instance, whether anyone ever rose a stronger or a wiser man from reading a number of the *Rambler* or a page of *Rasselas*; but we are quite sure that no one left Dr. Johnson's company without feeling that his moral constitution had been braced up. Dr. Jowett's translations of Plato and Thucydides are models of what a crib should be, for they manage to preserve the spirit of Greek and the style of English. But though their public may be increased by the spread of middle-class education, it is not on those works that the fame of their author rested or ever will rest. Jowett's influence was derived from his talk, at his own table, in his study, in the Balliol quadrangle, in his rambles round the Malvern Hills, with undergraduates, and with men of the world.

He had as shrewd an eye for an undergraduate as a Yorkshireman has for a horse, and he spotted his Milners, his Asquiths and his Curzons, with the certainty born of practice. If he trained his winners with more assiduity than his crocks, who shall blame him? Not that he could not be very kind to some of his shabbier pupils, but he was not so to all, and on industrious mediocrity he refused to waste his time. Jowett was often accused of "tuft-hunting", of paying more attention to undergraduates of social position than to the Browns, Joneses and Robinsons, and of preferring the company of the great ones of the earth. This was not due to snobbishness, but to his intuitive grasp of the realities of life, for, as he once said in a sermon, "Rank is not a dispensation of Providence, but it is a fact". There was another, and quite harmless, explanation of his undoubted preference for those whose manners were easy.

When he began his career at the Master's Lodge, Jowett was unaccustomed to society, and a little ill at ease; indeed, he never quite lost his shyness. He therefore liked people who were not afraid of him, fashionable women who rattled, undergraduates who "cheeked" him in the well-bred, Etonian way. To intellectual fear he was a stranger; and he would tackle Lord Salisbury, Mr. Gladstone or Matthew Arnold with equal intrepidity.

What was the secret of his personal influence? As in the case of Johnson, Jowett's conversation (in which we include his letters) drew its power from an extraordinary, and apparently intuitive insight into human life and character. There is no more wonderful faculty possessed by genius of a certain kind than that of seeing into and through phases of life of which it can have no experience.

Anthony Trollope, when he wrote *Barchester Towers*, was a Post Office inspector, who had never set foot, except casually, in a cathedral close. The advice Johnson gave to Boswell about practising at the Bar might have come from the oldest bencher in the Temple. Jowett had this gift of worldly intuition in a remarkable degree, and the science of life was with him a passion. When, therefore, he gave counsel to one of his favourite pupils or to an intimate friend, the hearer was immediately struck by its incisive shrewdness. This quality of worldly wisdom comes out very strongly in his letters to Sir Robert Morier, who was one of his few close friends. Take, for example, this passage from a letter to the celebrated diplomatist:

If I might advise (positively for the last time) on this joyful occasion, I would urge upon you once more "caution and reticence". I do not mean as to keeping of secrets, and I know that there must be a give and take of information. But what you do not appear to me to see is, that you cannot speak indiscriminately against Gladstone, Harcourt and other persons, who are for the moment influential, without raising a great deal of prejudice against yourself, and creating unnecessary drawbacks in the accomplishment of objects which you have at heart. Everyone knows how another speaks of him, and cannot be expected to love his assailant. Everybody acknowledges your ability, but I believe that the persons whose opinions you most value, feel that this defect of which you never seem to be aware has nearly shipwrecked you. May I give you as a motto for a diplomatist my favourite sentence out of Fielding: "I forgave him, not from any magnanimity of soul, still less from Christian charity, but simply because it was expedient for me". Or, to put the thought in a more unworldly phrase, I forgave him simply because, having the interests of England and

Europe at heart, I have no room for personal enmities or antipathies.

Sounder advice was surely never addressed to a rising man with a bitter tongue. Or take this sentence from a letter to Lord Lansdowne:

Measures of precaution are never justly appreciated, because when most effectual they are never seen to be necessary.

It is only when thought over that the profound and mellow wisdom of this saying is apparent. Or consider this passage from another letter to the same correspondent:

I want to urge upon you that the real time for making a reputation and gaining a position in politics is when you are out of office. Then you have independence and can act for yourself, and can make a carefully prepared speech. The difference between a man who has made a remarkable speech, whether in or out of Parliament, is enormous. To do it requires not natural eloquence, but a great deal of nerve, great industry, and familiar knowledge of a subject, and feeling about it. I do really believe that for a politician no pains can be too great about speaking. An important speech should be written out two or three times, and never spoken exactly as it was written. When once a person has gained the power of saying a few words in a natural manner to a large audience, he can hardly write too much.

Yet Jowett had no practical experience of diplomacy or politics.

So much has already been said and written of Jowett's sermons that one has no inclination to say much of him as a divine. Sydney Smith said he went to Church because it was his trade; and though Jowett was a militant member of the Broad Church his heart was never in theological controversy. He went to church at Malvern because he was a clergyman; but when he was bored by the sermon of the local pastor, he would calmly take out a pocket-book and make notes about Plato or Thucydides. *"Noscitur e sociis"* is as true in religious matters as in anything else, and Hang-Theology Rogers was one of Jowett's cronies. He is quite cross with Sir Robert Morier for proposing to write a book about Dr. Döllinger and the New Catholics.

There is no harm [he writes] in entering a little into religious controversy. You have had great opportunities of learning, and no doubt the friendship of such a man as Döllinger is well worth having. But I would rather write about great questions of European policy or social life. The New Catholic movement is nothing, or very

43

little, but Bismarck is a great deal, whether the time has come for him to descend from earth or not.

That is as characteristic of the man as anything in his correspondence. Great questions of European policy or social life are what he would be at; a religious movement is nothing to him. Dr. Johnson was violently agitated by the suggestion that had he gone to the Bar he would have been Lord Chancellor. It may be questioned whether a keen man of the world like Jowett was happy as a college don. If it is possible to judge from letters and after-dinner talk, he was quite contented. He had the serenity which comes from clearness and balance of mind, and if he was only a spectator, he had the satisfaction of knowing that many of the leading actors had learnt their parts from him.

IV

MR. "JIM" LOWTHER

IV

MR. "JIM" LOWTHER

LORD BEACONSFIELD said many years ago that to be in the House of Commons without being in London Society was like playing a game of blind-man's-buff.

The saying is no longer as true as it was. Society, by increasing its size, has diminished its power, and it is nowadays obliged to share a lessened influence with a well-informed Press. Everyone can mention several instances of men who have worked their way to the front rank in politics without any assistance from society. But there is still a great deal of truth left in the observation, for in every popular assembly the fact of a man's being in the social swim will always confer upon him a certain prestige.

Mr. James Lowther was "in the swim", and a good deal of his peculiar influence and position in the House of Commons was due to the knowledge that he was as much at home at Newmarket and Marlborough House as at Westminster. Even those Englishmen who know as little about the pasterns of a horse as Dr. Johnson have an unbounded respect for a Steward of the Jockey Club. A wealthy bachelor, "Jim" Lowther knew everybody, heard everything, went where he liked, and said what he pleased. Yet he was never known to abuse a confidence or a friend.

And this leads me to note that, apart from the *cachet* of his position on the turf and in society, Mr. James Lowther had moral qualities which are all too rare, but which never fail to secure their possessor the respect of his acquaintances and the affection of his friends. Mr. Lowther was as straight as a die; he was absolutely truthful; he knew no fear; he was perfectly loyal to his associates, whether in business or pleasure. But he expected other people to treat him as he treated them, and the writer remembers his complaining of the desertion of a colleague who had promised to support him in moving some amendment or resolution. "I have seen some shabby tricks played on the turf in my day", said Mr. Lowther sadly, "but I really cannot remember anything more shabby than Wharton's not turning up this afternoon."

He never forgot or dropped anybody. For a great many years Mr. Lowther used to invite some two dozen of his Parliamentary friends to an annual dinner at his house in Grosvenor Street or at the Bachelors' Club. Naturally, a good many of his original guests fell out of Parliament; but Mr. Lowther, though he added to his list, never struck off a name, and went on inviting and receiving the ex-M.P. with as much cordiality as if he was still an active and important colleague. His good breeding and self-possession never failed him in any company, and if he seldom said a witty thing, he never said a rude one.

There is a French proverb that it takes a bad heart to say a good thing, and in conversation Mr. Lowther was shrewd and sympathetic rather than brilliant. He never tried to score off anybody, knowing well the danger of the habit. He sometimes rambled a little in narrative, but his voice was so melodious and so well modulated that his listener was not fatigued. His exquisite courtesy and consideration for other people's feelings were based on something better than training—namely, on real kindness of nature. Such a man is bound to be loved. He was probably the recipient of a good many confidences, for he was just "the man of the world" whom men and women would consult in a difficulty. He was rather like Lord Eskdale in *Coningsby*, who is said to have been the Lord Lonsdale of Disraeli's youth.

In public life the position of Mr. James Lowther was unique. He had been Under-Secretary for the Colonies and Irish Secretary under Lord Beaconsfield; but no one remembers what he did in those posts; one never thought of him as an official. Jim Lowther was a personage in the country and in Parliament; but it was as a thoroughgoing Tory, not as a Front-Bencher, that he loomed large in the public eye.

Apart from the question of Protection, Mr. Lowther approached politics in a spirit of good-humoured indifference. For though he had a quaint habit of speaking of men of light and leading as "damned scoundrels", and generally referring to them as unconvicted felons, the abuse was purely Johnsonian, and the strange oaths and epithets were spoken so pleasantly that not even their subjects could have been offended. Once Mr. Lowther was caught in this way, for coming up from Margate in the train he was drawn into conversation by a fellow-passenger, to whom he confided that "old Sarum was a poop-stick" and "Balfour was a funker" and "Joe Chamberlain was" etc. etc. The traveller was aghast at hearing his member speak of these awful persons in this strain, and the conversation found its way into some newspaper.

Mr. Lowther was quite aware that he was regarded by his countrymen as the type of narrow-minded Tory squire, and was not above occasionally playing up or down to the part. Thus, although he spoke French unusually well for an Englishman, and was a frequent visitor to Paris, in addressing his Yorkshire or Kentish farmers he always alluded to the Frenchman as "Mounser" and if he had occasion to mention a French statesman by name he would say "Mounser Delcassy".

I recollect once crossing from Paris to London with Mr. Lowther, and from the moment we landed at Dover no royal prince or Prime Minister could have been treated with more signs of respect and good-will than the member for the Isle of Thanet. Guards walked before him to his carriage with bows and smiles, and when we got to Victoria some high official rushed into the Customs House and bawled out, "Pass Mr. James Lowther's luggage through at once!" All this was of course perfectly unsolicited and

51

unexpected attention, for there never was a simpler, a more unaffected and a less exacting man. It was an unbought tribute of sympathy and admiration from plain Britons to a character which they thoroughly appreciate, that of an upright, open-handed, free-spoken English gentleman, who did as he would be done by, and served his country to the best of his ability.

He certainly was no orator; in fact, he was a bad speaker, for he hummed and hawed a good deal from lack of vocabulary and from a not too copious flow of ideas. He was not above employing the arts of obstruction, for he considered everything was fair in war. And few could obstruct more artistically than Mr. James Lowther, for he knew his procedure at one time almost as well as Mr. Tim Healy, and he was always so polite that he did not excite the wrath of the Chair, or even of those against whom he was manœuvring.

Probably no one was less surprised than Mr. Lowther by Mr. Chamberlain's conversion to Protection. Either he had earlier information than the world, or the wish was father to the thought, for he was always darkly prophesying the event. He was a characteristic figure, and belonged to the régime which has long since passed away.

The type has gone, but has anything better, or as good, taken its place? The modern M.P. is a very different person from Jim Lowther, more earnest possibly, better educated in the Whitehall sense of the term. But is he as representative of the majority of his countrymen? I doubt it much.

V

LORD RANDOLPH CHURCHILL
AS SEEN BY HIS SON

V

LORD RANDOLPH CHURCHILL
AS SEEN BY HIS SON

APART from its intrinsic merits, which are great, this biography [1] is invested with an adventitious interest by the fact that Mr. Winston Churchill wrote it as a member of the Conservative Party, and published it as a member of the Liberal Party. It is not improbable that the lesson of his father's life sank deep into the son's mind, and that the tragedy and failure of it were the causes which impelled him to change his party. I hazard this remark because Mr. Churchill writes on page 448 (the chapter on the Parnell Commission): "But let it be observed that Lord Randolph Churchill was beaten, whatever he did, when he played the national game; and was victorious, whatever he did, while he played the party game. No question of 'taste' or 'patriotism' was raised when what he said, however outrageous, suited

[1] Winston Churchill, M.P., *Lord Randolph Churchill.*

his party. No claim of truth counted when what he said, however incontrovertible, was awkward for his party." This is but too true. He was that familiar figure in history since the days of Alcibiades, an aristocrat with strong democratic sympathies. He was vehemently anti-Jingo in foreign politics, and as early as 1877 tried to get up an intrigue with Sir Charles Dilke against Lord Beaconsfield's Turkish policy, actually offering to propose in the House of Commons the establishment of republics in Bulgaria and Herzegovina! In Egyptian politics he supported Wilfrid Blunt and Arabi Pacha, and in short was the champion of "oppressed nationalities". In home politics Lord Randolph Churchill was frankly Radical, favouring graduated taxation and enfranchisement of leaseholds. All this he called Tory Democracy: the democracy was plain enough, but where was the Toryism? Lord Randolph would have been happier and more successful if he had joined the Radical Party before 1880. Had he adhered to Mr. Gladstone in 1886 he would certainly have been his successor. If he had gone with Mr. Chamberlain and Lord Hartington, his position as a Radical Unionist would have been unassailable. But Lord Randolph Churchill's en-

vironment was too much for him. His defection
to the Radicals would have been a grievous blow
to those whom he loved and wished to please.
Once he broke out when his father was Viceroy
of Ireland in an anti-coercionist speech (1877),
and the Duke of Marlborough wrote to the Chief
Secretary: "My dear Beach—The only excuse I can
find for Randolph is, that he must either be mad,
or have been singularly affected with local champagne or claret". Towards the end of his life Lord
Randolph Churchill was fond of saying, "I don't
believe in dooks: I've seen too much of 'em". But
at the beginning of his life the ducal influence
was strong. When the Duke of Marlborough died
in 1883 Lord Randolph was in the full swing of
his opposition to the Gladstonian Government,
and three years later came the Home Rule Bill.
It is the old story of the missed opportunity. If
I am right in supposing that Mr. Winston
Churchill, meditating deeply on all these things,
as the drama of his father's life unfolded itself
beneath his eyes, determined not to miss his
opportunity, I cannot blame him. Indeed, I congratulate him on his decision to leave, before it was
too late, a party with which he was in imperfect
sympathy. He is the only instance I know, in life

or literature, of a son who has profited by the mistakes of his father.

I do not agree with Mr. Churchill that Lord Randolph reached the meridian of his intellectual power after he left the Government in December 1886. The highest point in his political life was touched, in my opinion, between 1880 and 1885, when Lord Randolph was beating down Mr. Gladstone in the House of Commons and building up the Tory Party in the big towns. Mr. Gladstone had emerged from the Midlothian campaign with a halo of glory such as never before or since surrounded the head of statesman. Gladstone-worship was rampant, and Lord Randolph Churchill was determined to break it down. Events favoured his enterprise, for neyer was Prime Minister so unlucky as Mr. Gladstone. It was a strange trick of fortune that a man of Mr. Gladstone's intense piety and scholarly refinement should have been compelled to throw the aegis of his eloquence over a blatant atheist like Bradlaugh. Bradlaugh was the foundation-stone of the Fourth Party, which found plenty of work for its hands in South Africa, in Egypt and in Ireland. A peace-loving Minister, who detested foreign and Colonial politics of every description, found

himself dragged into a South African war ending
in Majuba Hill; into Egyptian complications in-
volving the suppression of Arabi, the bombard-
ment of Alexandria, the abortive Soudan disaster,
the mission and murder of Gordon; and into a
species of civil war with Parnell and the Land
League in Ireland. Not a single point escaped
Lord Randolph Churchill, and with the eye of a
born tactician, he so selected his topics of attack
that he managed to enlist a certain amount of
Radical support for his most furious onslaughts
on the Government. At the same time he waged
a kind of left-handed war against his own leader
in the House of Commons, Sir Stafford Northcote. It is a most interesting historical fact that
Lord Beaconsfield confided to Sir John Gorst that
he would never have taken a peerage and left Sir
Stafford Northcote to lead the House of Commons, if he had not believed that Gladstone
meant what he said when he announced his retirement in 1874. That Lord Randolph's treatment
of Sir Stafford Northcote was marked by brutality
cannot be gainsaid. Disraeli's attacks on Sir
Robert Peel were also brutal. Men climb to the
topmost place in politics on the bodies of their
comrades. As the first Lord Halifax observed,

"State business is a cruel trade; good-nature is a bungler in it". The capture of the "machine", the National Union of Conservative Associations, completed Lord Randolph's triumph over the "old gang" or the "goats", as the Fourth Party nicknamed that trio of worthies, Sir Stafford Northcote, Sir Richard Cross and Mr. W. H. Smith. At the same time the brilliant guerilla chief became the idol of provincial platforms. Lord Randolph's speech at Blackburn in 1884 (the "chips" speech) will bear comparison with some of Disraeli's happiest exhibitions of satire and invective. This was the greatest period of Lord Randolph Churchill's career. He was the Conservative Party at that hour. When Conservatism was fast degenerating into old-fogyism and fat obstruction, Lord Randolph rehabilitated it by his own genius, breathed into its nostrils the breath of a popular movement, and made it a victorious force in the workshops of the artisans. If the borough franchise had not been extended to the agricultural labourers in 1884 there can be no doubt that the Conservatives would have swept the board in 1885, and, as it was, they captured the big towns, driving the Radicals into Boeotia. Strong as was the national feeling against Home

Rule, I do not believe that the Unionist majority in 1886 would have been anything like so large had it not been for Lord Randolph Churchill's conquest of the centres of industry between 1880 and 1885.

His abiding title to a place amongst statesmen is that he made Conservatism popular with the working classes, as only Disraeli had done before and as possibly no one will ever do again.[1] Suddenly in 1885 the successful rebel was converted into the suave and dignified Secretary of State for India, a post which he held for six months. We have Sir Arthur Godley's testimony that Lord Randolph was one of the best Secretaries of State who ever ruled the India Office. And I can easily believe it, for he was industrious, and far too clever not to know what he did not know. Nothing distinguishes a first-rate man from a second-rate man more sharply than the former's trust in skilled subordinates as contrasted with the latter's fussy suspicions. After the

[1] "Lord Randy", as the working men used to call him, was very popular with the masses. Between the highest and the lowest class there is what Thackeray called "a common bond of blackguardism". The middle class is regarded as an enemy by both.

election of 1886 Lord Randolph Churchill became Chancellor of the Exchequer and Leader of the House of Commons. Although the autumn session of that year was too short a time to test his real quality, Lord Randolph led with dignity, firmness and courtesy. His knowledge of the world enabled him to manage a mixed assembly, and although he sometimes rebuked a follower in private rather roughly, in the House he was conciliation itself. It was in December that the crash came. The crux of the situation was that Lord Randolph required the reduction of the Admiralty and War Office estimates by £1,300,000. Mr. W. H. Smith and Lord George Hamilton, in the most friendly and argumentative letters, wrote that they could not see their way to being responsible for the reductions demanded. Lord Salisbury was of course appealed to, and whilst negotiations were still in progress, the Chancellor of the Exchequer wrote from Windsor Castle on December 20, 1886, to the Prime Minister tendering his resignation, which Lord Salisbury accepted on the 22nd, and on the 23rd the news was in *The Times*. Even at the time Lord Randolph's friends were aghast, and he received an extremely sensible letter of advice from Mr. Labouchere, in which the following sentence occurs: "I should have thought that your game was rather a waiting one. Sacrifice everything to becoming a fetish: then, and only then, you can do as you like." But to wait and submit himself to others were the two things which Lord Randolph Churchill was temperamentally incapable of doing; and from the day when the world discovered this fact, it turned its back on him. Other Ministers have resigned and increased their popularity; but Lord Randolph lost a great deal more than office: he parted with the confidence of men. He made two miscalculations of so gross a character as to be almost unintelligible. He thought himself indispensable, and he believed economy to be popular in practice, whereas it is only popular in theory. After his resignation Lord Randolph Churchill made several good speeches from his corner seat behind the Treasury bench, and on one great question he was indisputably right and the Government wrong. The appointment of the Parnell Commission was both unconstitutional and impolitic. It is a sound maxim that an extraordinary tribunal should never be set up to try an issue which could be tried by the ordinary courts. As a political move it was a gross blunder, because the Unionists would have gained more by taunting Parnell with his fear of a British jury than they gained by the report of the judges, which produced no result. The election of 1892 threw the Conservatives into Opposition, and drew them together again. Lord Randolph Churchill was once more received into favour, and resumed his seat on the Front Bench. But it was too late. The speech on the disestablishment of the Welsh Church was the last leap of a dying fire. The blithe and debonair Lord Randolph was transformed at forty-five into a paralytic dotard, struggling heroically with a pitiless Até. His friends and relatives were unable to prevent him making platform speeches; "but the crowds who were drawn by the old glamour of his name departed sorrowful and shuddering at the spectacle of a dying man, and those who loved him were consumed with embarrassment and grief". In these words Mr. Churchill describes one of the most tragic ends in history.

VI

LORD CURZON

VI

LORD CURZON[1]

IN the name of biography, as a serious branch of history and letters, I protest with all my might against rushing "the authorised biography" of a great man on to the public within two years of his death. The first volume of Mr. Buckle's *Life of Disraeli* was not published until 1910, nineteen years after his death. Lady Gwendolen Cecil published the first two volumes of her father's biography in 1921, eighteen years after his death, and she stopped at 1881. Lord Morley, who ought to have known better, began this habit of hustling the dead into the limelight before their bones were cold by producing his three volumes on Gladstone in 1903, the fifth year from the funeral in Westminster Abbey. The case is different when a man publishes his autobiography during his lifetime. He is asking for trouble, and deserves all he gets, for himself, his relatives and his friends. But I can see no excuse for Lord Curzon's literary

[1] Rt. Hon. the Earl of Ronaldshay, *The Life of Lord Curzon*.

executors, or for Lord Ronaldshay, unless it be the frenzied hurry of our day, and the fear that their friend will be forgotten in a decade, a poor compliment to Lord Curzon. As it is, the criticism must be candied rather than candid, which is not the historical method. I shall inevitably offend friends, relatives and admirers; but the fault is not mine.

Lord Ronaldshay is well qualified for the task of Lord Curzon's biographer. Seventeen years younger than his hero, Lord Ronaldshay has followed, I will not say *longo intervallo*, in his footsteps. He has served many years in the House of Commons; he has travelled much in the Far East; he was Lord Curzon's aide-de-camp during the viceroyalty; he was Governor of Bengal; by his books he has shown himself to be a man of wide and discriminating culture. Yet he has betrayed a lack of one literary quality, the sense of perspective. The hundred pages he has devoted to George Curzon's Eton and Balliol days might well have been compressed into thirty. The school and college life of clever and precocious youths, born with a silver spoon in their mouth, is very much the same. Of the Presidents of Pop and the Union, of the winners of prizes and fellowships, not five per cent. make good in after-life, probably less in these democratic times.

Since Lord Ronaldshay has lingered at such length upon Oxford, I will quote two sentences from that period, which prove how true it is that the boy is father to the man. Commenting on George Curzon's Lothian Essay, Dean Kitchin wrote to Raper that it was marred by "a certain pretentiousness of style and character". That stuck to Curzon all his life. In his rooms in the Garden Quad a cracked teapot was placed on the table. The scout had a blameless record of forty years' service, which did not shield him from being haled before Jowett by the furious George. The unpleasant truth is that never in his long and varied life did Curzon learn how to treat servants properly. Nor was it only servants, but all who were his subordinates, that he bullied. At the Foreign Office in his last years the "Markiss" was detested, and when Mr. Ramsay MacDonald took his place, the clerks said, "Thank heaven!" Lord Ronaldshay does not conceal this defect of temper, but apologises for it by saying that "He expected others to exhibit the same efficiency in the discharge of their duties as he displayed himself". That will not do, though everyone agrees that Curzon never spared himself in the matter of hard work. But the Chief does his work in the rarefied air of Olympus, at his own time, and amid all the luxurious surroundings of wealth. The clerk, the official, the footman, work in very different conditions. A much better defence of his manners would have been the state of his health, which was so bad all through his life as to excuse irritability, though not want of consideration for others.

Lord Ronaldshay tells us that Lord Curzon always paid more attention to style than to matter. Lord Morley was a great admirer of Lord Curzon's form as a speaker, I suppose because it was the antithesis of his own. Curzon's style, both in speaking and writing, was Corinthian, of which, according to Matthew Arnold, the characteristic is that "it has no soul; all it exists for is to get its end, to make its points, to damage its adversaries, to be admired, to triumph". That, as a public man, was Lord Curzon. In private life he was said to be tender, affectionate, humorous, loyal to his friends, bubbling over with gaiety. These virtues are revealed in the testimony of a crowd of contemporaries, in his correspondence at this period with Mr. St. John Brodrick, and in the romance of his long love, his secret engagement and his marriage with Mary Leiter.

In 1885 George Curzon, as the eldest son of Lord Scarsdale, and heir to Kedleston, contested South Derbyshire, where he was defeated by the newly enfranchised miners. In 1886 he found a safe seat at Southport, the fashionable suburb of Liverpool, which he continued to represent until he left for India in 1898. For the greater part of the time, instead of hanging about the House of Commons, gossiping in the Lobby, or trying to catch the Speaker's eye, Curzon roamed all over the world, specialising, as we should say, in journalese, in Persia, Central Asia and India. In the last year of Lord Salisbury's second administration Curzon was appointed to succeed Brodrick as Under-Secretary for India. During the nine months that he dealt with Indian affairs in this subordinate capacity nothing of note occurred to evoke his powers of debate, except a couple of easy victories over Mr. Swift MacNeill, and the introduction of an Indian Council's Bill, which nobody took the slightest interest in, and which was a sort of mild prelude to the subsequent reforms of Lords Morley and Minto. Followed the three years' interlude of the Liberal Government; their defeat by Mr. Brodrick on the obscure subject of cordite; the formation in 1895 of Lord Salisbury's third Government, Curzon's marriage to the lovely daughter of the Chicago millionaire, and his appointment to the post of Under-Secretary for Foreign Affairs.

Then it was that Curzon began to show his true metal, his courage, his power of debate and his vigorous Imperialism. The times abroad were ticklish, not to say dangerous. Both France and Germany wanted to quarrel with England, but dared not. They pursued, both of them, a policy of pin-pricks which Lord Salisbury, who was both Prime Minister and Foreign Secretary, suffered with a patience that his young Under-Secretary in the Commons found hard to defend. Not that he did not make a good defence in the House. On the contrary, all his dexterity and his glittering eloquence were thrown into his speeches, which he delivered with much scorn of his opponent, and occasional slappings on the box. Privately, however, he wrote earnest letters of remonstrance to Lord Salisbury, which differed much from those of Lord Randolph Churchill in that they were always deferential, and even affectionate. The Under-Secretary was ever in favour of standing up to both Germany and France, and he hated the French Colonial official. On one occasion he wrote to his Chief as follows:

I can well see the advantage of a bargain, and I have surmised that such was the object of a conciliatory attitude towards France. But they seem a little reluctant to reciprocate generosity. It is all take, and very little give with them.

Lord Salisbury treated Curzon, of whom he was genuinely fond, as a father would treat a wayward boy. The Under-Secretary's protests did not deflect the Foreign Secretary from his policy by a hair's-breadth. The fact is that Lord Salisbury was an incorrigible realist. He did not believe that England would go to war for any question short of the defence of her shores. Consequently he had no foreign policy with regard to China, Japan, France or Germany; or to put it in a different light, Lord Salisbury's foreign policy was concentrated in the Concert of Europe, which was the nineteenth-century equivalent to the League of Nations. It is, I think, very creditable both to Curzon and the Prime Minister that, knowing well that the younger man belonged to the forward school of Imperialists, both in Europe and on the

Indian frontier, Lord Salisbury should have appointed him Viceroy of India.

The most malignant deity could not have devised a more fatal gift for George Curzon than his appointment at the age of thirty-nine to the Viceroyalty of India. The boyish idolatry of Eton, followed by the flattery of Balliol, both rather unpleasant samples of snobbishness, would soon have been corrected by the back benches of the House of Commons, if the leaders of his party had left Curzon to fight his way to the front. But he was thrust into a post which excited and confirmed the worst faults of his character. The Viceroy of India is the nearest thing to an absolute monarch which the British Empire tolerates. For seven years Curzon was on a pedestal with no one to say him nay. Then he was confronted by a man with a will and a conceit as strong as his own. The Home Government, whom the Governor-General had sorely tried, supported Kitchener, and Curzon returned in something like disgrace. Yet he could not understand why he was not received with banquets, and why the Garter and a peerage were not conferred on him by a Liberal Premier.

His first contact with the reality of politics came in 1911 over the Parliament Act. Curzon

began, as he always did in those days, by contemptuous laughter at his opponents. The idea
that Asquith would create 500 peers was "fan-
tastic"—I can hear him saying it. His next stage,
as always, was furious opposition; and his last,
surrender. He urged the Conservative peers to
vote against the Government; then to absent themselves with Lansdowne; and finally I do not remember whether he voted with the Government, or
abstained, and Lord Ronaldshay leaves the point
obscure. Several Conservative peers were so en-
raged by Curzon's cowardice that they voted for
the Bill. This transaction damaged Curzon's
chances of leading his party.

In May 1915 Asquith formed his coalition, and
Curzon was brought into the Cabinet with the
nominal office of Lord Privy Seal. For the first
time he sat and worked with experienced politicians, some of whom were his superiors.
Occasionally he made himself ridiculous. When it
was a question of evacuating the Gallipoli penin-
sula, the Lord Privy Seal adjourned the Cabinet
that he might read a memorandum on the horrors
of the Sicilian expedition under Nikias as translated by Grote from Thucydides!

The intrigue by which Asquith was forced to

resign at the end of 1916 has been described by many pens. The triumvirate of conspirators were Mr. Lloyd George, Bonar Law and Lord Beaver-brook. Behind them, aiding and abetting, were many Conservative leaders, Lords Carson and Balfour, I suppose, for two, and was Lord Curzon among them? Some part he must have played: Lord Ronaldshay ignores the business. Before this deplorable transaction, Curzon became President of the Air Board, and was so elated that he attacked the Admiralty, of which Mr. Balfour was First Lord. More than ten years had elapsed since the row about Kitchener, but George ought not to have forgotten Arthur's rapier-play. "I do not suppose", wrote the First Lord on Curzon's memorandum, "that in the whole history of the country any Government Department has ever indulged so recklessly in the luxury of inter-departmental criticism. The temptation has no doubt existed; but it has been more or less success-fully resisted. In the case of the Air Board, how-ever, the ardour of youth and the consciousness of superior abilities have completely broken through the ordinary barriers of self-restraint." That was only one of many reminders that he was no longer at Simla that the ex-Viceroy was to receive.

Curzon's conduct over the female enfranchisement clause in the Reform Act of 1918 was not only treacherous but imbecile. He had become in Mr. Lloyd George's first Ministry Lord President of the Council and Leader of the House of Lords. He was also President of the Anti-Suffrage League, as being the most eminent and bitter opponent of women's votes. As usual, Curzon began by throwing himself into frenzied opposition. Then as the time drew near, he began to shirk, and told the Anti-Suffrage League that as Leader of the House of Lords he could not vote against the clause. Lord Loreburn moved the rejection of the clause in Committee, and Lord Curzon said that the proposal would introduce "a vast, incalculable and almost catastrophic change", without precedent and without justification. "If your lordships pass this part of the Bill, you are doing more than crossing the Rubicon—you are opening the floodgates to a stream which for good or evil will submerge many landmarks we have known." He then announced that he would not vote against the clause, because it had been inserted by an overwhelming majority of the House of Commons! That is exactly the attitude he took up four years later on the Bill for giving effect to the Montagu-

Chelmsford Report on Indian Government. One would have thought that on India at all events Curzon would have stiffened his back. But no, he pointed out from his expert knowledge the folly and dangers of Montagu's crude proposals—which the Simon Commission later tried to modify—and concluded, with a shrug of the shoulders and a vote for the Bill, that according to democratic ideas it was better for a people to be badly governed by themselves than well governed by a superior power! If this is the philosophy of the House of Lords, in God's name of what use is it?

The whole story of Lord Curzon's position as Foreign Secretary in Mr. Lloyd George's Government between 1918 and 1922 is humiliating, if not shameful. Lord Ronaldshay cannot find room to tell us what Curzon thought of the surrender to murder and treason in Ireland, of the treaty with Collins and Griffith to break Pitt's Union. Curzon may have sheltered himself behind Lord Birkenhead and Sir Austen Chamberlain, and said that Ireland was not his department. But foreign affairs were his department. And there is not one of the many disastrous policies forced upon a docile Parliament by Mr. Lloyd George, the crime of the war against Turkey into which

Greece was egged by England and France, the Mesopotamia folly, the scuttle out of Egypt, the trading agreement with Russia, to which the Foreign Secretary did not object. The process was always the same; objections, protest by memorandum, and acquiescence. It came to be known that Curzon would not resign, and when that is known about a Minister, his counsel loses authority, and he is looked upon by his chief as a serviceable tool. Curzon would not resign because he suffered from the delusion that he was indispensable, or because he was afraid of letting in a rival.

The painful scene with Lord Stamfordham, in 1923, when the King's preference for Mr. Baldwin was communicated to Curzon, is given with the latter's pencilled *cri de cœur*. Whether King George acted constitutionally in sending for Mr. Baldwin without consulting Mr. Bonar Law, and whether His Majesty was right in saying that a Prime Minister in the House of Lords was an impossibility, are questions that cannot be discussed here. The King was, at all events, following his grandmother's precedent in 1894.

VII

SIR HENRY FOWLER
(VISCOUNT WOLVERHAMPTON)

SIR HENRY FOWLER
(VISCOUNT WOLVERHAMPTON)

FOWLER, Ritchie and W. H. Smith were the political products of that great middle class which ruled England from the death of Lord Palmerston in 1865 to Mr. Gladstone's death at the close of the nineteenth century. Some would add Gladstone and Peel to the list, but they would be wrong, for those two statesmen were of Eton and Christ Church; they never were engaged in any trade or profession, and belonged distinctly to the upper middle class.

As for Disraeli, he was an exotic, and belonged to no class but the very tiny one of genius. Fowler, Ritchie and W. H. Smith were the quintessence of the Victorian middle class, and between them there was a strong family likeness in manners, appearance and modes of thought and expression—all were intensely serious, methodical and inclined to be pompous. But Henry Fowler was head and shoulders above the other two in point of brains; for whereas Ritchie and Smith were dull because they had neither lucidity nor humour, Fowler was never dull, because he had lucidity, though he was quite devoid of humour.

How lamentably lacking he was in this "modulating and restraining balance-wheel", as Lowell called the sense of humour, is shown by a story which his gifted daughter tells against him. They were reading to him a passage from the proofs of *The Farringdons*—one of Miss Thorneycroft Fowler's novels, and they came upon the satirical description of a political climber and his young helpmeet. "Have they any children?" (asks someone in the novel). "No, only politics." Sir Henry Fowler laid down the sheets and underlined the word "no". "I shouldn't say that," he exclaimed gravely to the author, "it is too conclusive. I should say 'not yet'!" And Mrs. Hamilton assures us that her father could not understand why they all laughed so much! What is to be done with such a man?

Henry Fowler was the family solicitor to the Radical Party, and looked the part. He was an excellent adviser, for his judgement was sound and, having been bred an attorney, he was cautious, and knew the meaning of evidence. From another point of view, Sir Henry Fowler was one of those men, numerous enough in a reserved and shy nation, whose appearance and manner convey a very wrong impression of their inner nature. Sir Henry Fowler's carriage was severe, even to the point of being tinged with clericalism. His voice was loud and harsh, and his manner was dogmatic and domineering. Outwardly he was just what the French mean when they talk of *un homme cassant*. But in reality Henry Fowler was a warm, even tender-hearted, man, sympathetic, broad in his views, and tolerant of those who differed from him. He had all the bourgeois respect for rank, and was deferential and partial to Lord Randolph Churchill, an attitude which the young patrician civilly reciprocated. The elation which the provincial lawyer felt at being the Queen's guest at Balmoral and petted by the duchesses and maids of honour is expressed in his letters to his family with infantine frankness.

He was in partnership for a great many years with Sir Robert Perks, and they did a big solicitor's business, financing and directing large commercial schemes, with all the provincial Nonconformist interest behind them. This occupation gave Fowler a kind of training and experience that is always rare among politicians, even on the

Liberal side, and particularly rare on both front benches, whose occupants have, with few exceptions, been immersed from their youth in Parliamentary business, which is different from every other business in this world. In a commercial age nothing is more valuable to a statesman than personal familiarity with the routine and documents of business, bills of lading and exchange, deeds, and contracts of all kinds, from building agreements to charter-parties.

Sir Henry Fowler was thus peculiarly well equipped for the post of Financial Secretary to the Treasury, which he filled in the short Gladstone Government of 1886. In Gladstone's last Administration (1892–4) he was admitted to the Cabinet as President of the Local Government Board, and in Lord Rosebery's ill-starred Ministry he was for one year Secretary of State for India. This was the zenith of a long political career, which came rather late to fruition, for Sir Henry Fowler was then sixty-five, and his speech on the Indian cotton duties was his greatest achievement. It was a critical and important occasion, for the Lancashire members had been instructed by their constituents, irrespective of party, to oppose the Government. The import duties on cotton yarns and goods had been taken off by the Indian Government in 1882, as they were no longer needed for revenue. But in 1895, owing to the fall in the rupee, it was found necessary for revenue to re-impose the import duties, accompanied by a countervailing duty of excise on Indian cotton yarns and goods.

Sir Henry James was at that time member for Bury, and he led a powerful opposition from Lancashire to the duties. The rights and wrongs of the policy do not matter now, but Sir Henry Fowler made a very eloquent speech in defence of the Indian Government. He concluded with the words:

My right honourable friend has said that India has no representative in this House. I deny the accuracy of that allegation. The representatives of India in this House are not one or two individuals, not even the section of members who are thought to be experts on the one hand, or those men who have a profound, a deep, and a special interest in Indian affairs on the other. Every member of this House, whether elected by an English, or by a Scotch or by an Irish constituency, is a member for India. All the interests of India, personal, political, commercial, financial and social, are committed to the individual and collective responsibility of the House of Commons. I ask the

House to discharge that gigantic trust, uninfluenced by any selfish or party feeling, but with wisdom, and justice, and generosity.

This peroration, pronounced in a deep voice and with great emphasis, produced quite an unusual effect upon a cynical audience, and actually persuaded some of the Lancashire members to vote against Sir Henry James, whose motion was defeated by nearly three to one. Every public man has "one crowded hour of glorious life", and that was Henry Fowler's hour. He lived on that speech for the rest of his life, and shortly after the accession of the Radical Party to power in 1906 he was made Lord President of the Council, and glided away into the crimson shadows of the Upper House.

Just because Henry Fowler's type of manhood is no longer popular and powerful in the national life—indeed it may be doubted if it ever was popular, for it is not very amiable in public, whatever it may be in private—just because the provincial Nonconformist man of business, with his austerity and his angularity, is no longer the pattern of our days, we are apt to overlook the sterling qualities which underlie that character. Henry Fowler was a religious, truthful, brave, honest man, and he was an industrious and highly efficient Minister of State. He had no ear for music, nor eye for art; he was not a clubbable man: he was not socially graceful or entertaining, and he afforded a tempting target for the light-glancing wit of Mr. George Russell. Still, England owes something to the Puritan breed, which perhaps we can hardly do without.

VIII

SIR JOHN GORST

SIR JOHN GORST

SIR JOHN GORST'S career illustrates instructively the fate of a politician who cannot make himself a good party man. What measure of social or domestic happiness Sir John Gorst enjoyed I do not know, nor is it relevant. But for a man of first-rate mental calibre, his public life was an indisputable failure. Rebellion against the bonds of party was the chief, though not the only, cause of his want of success. He never obtained complete control of his temper; he was inflexible to a point which some call obstinacy, and others tenacity; and (unlike many other men) he never managed to combine his interest at the Bar with his interest in the House of Commons.

Instead of making the politician help the lawyer, and thus pursuing his advancement along parallel lines, he contrived to set the one against the other, and thus vulgarly speaking, he fell between two stools. Having emerged from the mathematical tripos as Third Wrangler, Gorst sailed for New Zealand, falling in love, like Warren Hastings, on the voyage, though, not like the pro-consul, with another man's wife.

In the Antipodes he seems to have dabbled in missionary work and journalism, returning to England in his thirtieth year, and being called to the Bar. A year after his call he got himself elected for the town of Cambridge, a most imprudent step from a professional point of view. Two years later, in 1868, he lost his seat, and at Disraeli's request he gave himself to the work of organising the Tory Party in the constituencies. In 1874 he certainly proved himself an organiser of victory, for he gave Disraeli the first and last majority of his life. And here Gorst's want of worldly wisdom, or capacity for self-advancement, first showed itself. In his hour of triumph Disraeli could have denied his Chief of Staff nothing. Gorst asked for nothing, not even a safe and comfortable seat. He stood at a by-election in 1875 for Chatham, at that time a troublesome, expensive and uncertain constituency.

Perhaps embittered by the lack of reward, which is never got in politics except for the asking, Gorst developed into the guerilla chief who became so famous in the Gladstonian Parliament of 1880. It was well known that Gladstone was more irritated by the "hon. and learned member for Chatham" than by any other of his many opponents, which is intelligible enough; for Gorst's speeches were not relieved by wit or eloquence, or humour, in which he was strangely deficient; they were cold and logical statements of the case.

The Fourth Party was as torn by domestic dissension as all political combinations. The late Mr. Staveley Hill told me that he once invited the Fourth Party to a dinner-party. "Arthur" could not or would not come, the fear of Uncle Salisbury being ever at the back of his head. The first of the remaining trio to arrive was Sir Henry Drummond Wolff, his natural suavity overcast by the scared and hunted look which he wore in those days. In his silkiest tones he said to his host, "If Gorst and Randolph are coming, don't put me near them, as our relations are rather strained".

Next arrived Sir John Gorst, who, fixing Drummond Wolff with his eyeglass, said in his cold and caustic tone, "My dear Hill, keep me away from Wolff, as we are not on speaking terms". Last arrived Lord Randolph Churchill, who rolled his prominent eyes round the room, and clutching his host's arm whispered fiercely, "I see you've got those damned fellows Wolff and

Gorst. For God's sake put me the other side of the table, as I hate the very sight of 'em." Staveley Hill, of course, laughed, and told them to sit where they liked as it was a man's dinner.

In the summer of 1885 the Fourth Party was dissolved in office, Randolph Churchill becoming Secretary of State for India and Gorst being made Solicitor-General, a post which was worth at that time ten or twelve thousand a year. As Gorst was a poor man with a large family, it might have been supposed that he was satisfied. On the contrary, he was, if not openly indignant, certainly fretful at being excluded from the Cabinet. Lord Salisbury's first Government was turned out six months later, in February 1886, by Gladstone and the Parnellites. The first Home Rule Bill was rejected by the House of Commons in June 1886, and the general election gave Lord Salisbury a majority.

When forming his second Ministry Lord Salisbury offered Sir John Gorst the Solicitor-Generalship on the understanding that he would take the first puisne judgeship that fell vacant. Most political lawyers would say that this offer was generous payment for services to the Party. But Gorst refused it with asperity, and was finally appointed Under-Secretary for India with a salary of £1500! These are the facts, but I cannot say whether Gorst's refusal was due to perversity, or to a consciousness that he was unfitted for high legal office. He had never had any practice at the Bar: as he went into the House of Commons a year after being called it was impossible for him to get business as a junior.

The story was current at the Bar in 1885, though I cannot vouch for its truth, that one of the judges in the Court of Appeal exclaimed, "Mr. Solicitor, you are ignorant of the A B C of your business". This could not have been pleasant to the proud and fiery temper of Gorst, the less so because he must have known it to be true. But though he was not what is called a tradesman-lawyer, Gorst would probably have made a good judge; certainly some of his contemporaries who were promoted to the Bench knew quite as little law as he.

It was as Under-Secretary for India that I first came into contact with Sir John Gorst in the Parliament of 1886, and the occasion was interesting, as illustrating the extraordinary change of public opinion on a certain subject. The Cantonment Acts required the sanction of Parliament, and Mr. Walter M'Laren had put down a motion to repeal, or not to continue, the regulations for venereal disease. I asked Gorst in the Lobby what the Government were going to do, and he told me (very crossly) that they dared not oppose M'Laren's motion! I asked whether if I, as a private member, opposed M'Laren, and moved the continuance of the Acts, he would lend me the Government whips, and he very earnestly and kindly begged me not to injure my prospects by appearing as the champion of vice.

Thus was it proposed to sacrifice the health of our troops in India to Parliamentary hypocrisy, and I have lived to read the Report of the Royal Commission on Venereal Diseases![1] Gorst afterwards became Financial Secretary to the Treasury, and then Vice-President of the Education Committee. He was always in hot water, and always quarrelling with his chiefs. He was offered the post of High Commissioner of South Africa and refused it, because he would not abandon his ambition of entering the Cabinet.

Gorst cordially disliked Chamberlain and distrusted his methods. As Chamberlain was rapidly

[1] I believe the Government of India managed to evade or ignore the House of Commons vote.

dominating the Tory Party, Gorst threw up his office in 1902, and opposed the Protectionist propaganda. Of course, he lost his seat at Cambridge University in 1905, and then his genuine, if somewhat morbid, sympathy with the suffering of poverty, the fruit of his deep religious feelings, expressed itself in political socialism. He stood as a Radical in 1910 for his native town of Preston, and was beaten. His brother dying shortly afterwards, he succeeded to his estates, and ended his life as a Wiltshire squire. Sir John Gorst was a brave, conscientious, public-spirited man, with a first-class brain; but his disposition was froward, and was the main obstacle to his worldly success.

IX

HENRY LABOUCHERE

IX

HENRY LABOUCHERE

FEW men who have occupied no official position, filled so large a space in the public eye as Mr. Labouchere. He was indeed a rare combination of opposites. Belonging by birth to the upper class, and inheriting a large share in a Lancashire bank, he was an irreclaimable Bohemian and an advanced Radical. There is always something attractive about a man who, having been educated at Eton and Cambridge, and drawing £10,000 a year from bank shares, turns his back upon "the perfumed chambers of the great", and chooses to live with actors, journalists and republicans. He seems to have a leg in both worlds, and while he retails to mortals the scandals of Olympus he is thought to speak what he knows. If to this mode of life such a man adds the fearless denunciation, by tongue and pen, of abuses in high and low places, the attraction becomes influence and popularity.

Sir Francis Burdett played this game very well at the beginning of the nineteenth century, and Mr. Labouchere played it even better at its close, for he did not, like Sir Francis Burdett, turn Tory in his old age. The Laboucheres have been great people in the high finance of Amsterdam and in society at The Hague for more than a century. Henry eschewed the family trade of banking (except as a shareholder), and began life in the Diplomatic Service, where he was a thorn in the side of the Foreign Office. For Henry Labouchere was a born rebel; he could no more help being an Ishmael than he could help his decidedly Dutch physiognomy. His mind was of the irreverent, inquiring order which takes nothing for granted, and frequently assumes that everything established is an imposture. The exposure of humbugs and swindlers in all walks became the passion of Mr. Labouchere's life, and he rendered great service to society at considerable personal expense. There was not a begging-letter writer, or a bucket-shop keeper, or an extortionate moneylender, or a religious quack, or a fraudulent company promoter, or a purveyor of obscenity in any guise, who did not await the weekly issue of *Truth* with rage and trembling.

As an exposer of fraud Mr. Labouchere must have disbursed large sums, though I have no doubt the circulation of his paper recouped him. But innumerable libel actions are not defended for nothing, and there must have been a large detective staff; for information, as Lord Salisbury once said of our Secret Service fund, is entirely a question of money. Nor should it be forgotten in an enumeration of his service to the public that we owe it to Mr. Labouchere that Constitution Hill is now a public thoroughfare. "The courage of the man", as I once heard a speaker in Hyde Park exclaim, "in fighting the Queen, and all the bigwigs to open Constitution Hill!"

When we turn from the assailant of abuses and the terror of evildoers to the political journalist and member of Parliament, the record is blurred by extravagance and rabid partisanship. It is impossible that so clear-headed a man of the world as Mr. Labouchere can have believed all that he used to say and write of the Tory leaders. He once accused Lord Salisbury of helping a titled criminal to escape from a warrant, and of telling a lie to hide his connivance. He was, of course, instantly suspended by the Speaker, and it is more than probable that the ebullition was calculated. This was not the only time that Mr. Labouchere offended the taste of the House of Commons, for in 1881, when Mr. Gladstone pronounced a funeral eulogy on Lord Beaconsfield, Mr. Labouchere's attack on the policy and career of the dead statesman was drowned by murmurs from all sides.

With these two exceptions Mr. Labouchere managed very tactfully to assert the most violent opinions without making enemies of his brother members. There have been journalists in the House of Commons who earned their living by turning their colleagues into ridicule—a gross abuse of the freemasonry of Parliament. Mr. Labouchere was too well-bred, as well as too good-natured, to make this mistake. The leaders on both sides Mr. Labouchere considered fair game, but he never attacked private members, however prominent or obnoxious.

Like Abraham Lincoln, he had a weakness for repeating or inventing coarse stories, which were not always amusing, but made him a favourite of the smoking-room. This was the more exasperating as he was a really witty man.

Lord Taunton was his uncle, and someone, wishing to be agreeable, said, "Oh, Mr. Labouchere, I have just heard your father make an admirable speech in the House of Lords". "Really?" said Labouchere, "my father has been dead some years, and I always wondered where he had gone to." On the floor of the House of Commons "the Christian member for Northampton" made no effect whatever. His speeches were as a rule mere *réchauffés* of his articles in *Truth*, delivered in a languid drawl with the aid of bits of paper which he dropped one by one into his hat after use.

He once told me that he spoke to the reporters, and regarded his fellow-members as rows of lay figures. "Until you get into that frame of mind," he said, kindly enough, to a youngster not of his own side, "you will never succeed in politics." But it was with a stylo in his hand, and a cigarette-holder in his mouth, that Mr. Labouchere became great. The editor of *Truth* never got credit for the real excellence of his prose style simply because no one expects to meet with first-rate English in a society weekly. Mr. Labouchere used to write a great deal in his paper, sometimes "notes" and sometimes leaders. Though unsigned, his "copy" was unmistakable.

In directness, in simplicity, in terseness of wit and humour, Mr. Labouchere's prose was Voltairean: it was better than Cobbett's, for that great master of journalism spoiled his effects by exaggeration and violent vituperation. Good writing is so rare in the English Press that it is a thousand pities these articles should be lost.

Mr. Labouchere had another conspicuous foible: in the words of a French moralist, "*il faisait une fanfaronnade des vices, dont il n'était pas capable*". He took so low a view of his fellows that out of mere good-fellowship he was bound to make himself out as bad as he conceived them to be, or rather worse.

Once, after a rubber was over, his partner pointed out that his play, though successful, was extremely risky, as the adversary might have held such-and-such a card. "I agree," said Labouchere, "but then I took the precaution of looking over his hand."

When he was City editor of the *World* (his first essay in journalism) he tried operating on the Stock Exchange, and to help his speculation would write up the shares of which he was a bull, and write down the shares of which he was a bear. After he was caught at these manœuvres by the publication of some letters never intended for the light of day, Labouchere blandly asked, "What greater proof can I give of my belief in the shares I write up than buying them? Or what stronger evidence can there be of my disbelief in a share than my selling it?"

He soon gave up speculating, however, being much too clever not to realise that he could not play against the professional financier. In the Home Rule days, between 1886 and 1895, Mr. Labouchere was plunged in intrigue, and it was he who first saw through Pigott, and induced the forger to confess to Sir George Lewis and himself by means which his nephew, Mr. Thorold, has related to us in his interesting biography. The correspondence between Mr. Labouchere and Mr. Chamberlain on the Home Rule Bill of 1886 is not edifying. Both correspondents begin by treating the political situation as a problem in chess. But Mr. Chamberlain quickly drew off, and occupied high ground.

Labouchere makes no secret of the fact that he did not care a rap about Ireland and the Irish, but only wanted to get them out of the way:

For my part, I would coerce the Irish, grant them Home Rule, or do anything with them, in order to make the Radical programme possible. Ireland is but a pawn in the game. If they make fools of themselves, it would be easy to treat them as the North did the South, rule by the sword and suppress all representation.[1]

[1] Labouchere to Chamberlain, March 31, 1886, Thorold's *Life of Labouchere*, pp. 289-90.

What is almost incredible, but is true, is that this clear-sighted cynic, this laughing philosopher, who wrote himself down an unprincipled trifler, was really disappointed because Gladstone did not ask him to join his Cabinet in 1892, and genuinely offended because he was not, in the alternative, sent as Ambassador to Washington! The first refusal he put down to the Queen, and the second to Lord Rosebery, whom he pursued in *Truth* with unrelenting abuse. Such are the "follies of the wise"! Labouchere was what our neighbours used to call *très fin de siècle*; he was a very clever and amusing personality, whose withdrawal from politics and journalism left us all sadder men.

Mr. Bennett, the late editor of *Truth*, has told the public that his former editor-proprietor was perfectly indifferent as to what became of his copy after it had left his pen. When he retired to Florence, in the last years, he wrote much for his journal, but much of it was so irrelevant that it had to go into the waste-paper basket; yet Labouchere never complained, or perhaps did not perceive it. Few, very few of the touchy tribe of journalists achieve so serene a philosophy.

X

MR. SPEAKER PEEL

X

MR. SPEAKER PEEL

IT is impossible to write of the transition period in our politics without thinking at once of its presiding figure. Speaker Peel it was who guided from the Chair of the House of Commons—sorely against his will we may be sure—the transition from the traditional to the forceful method of transacting politics. Lord Beaconsfield observed that you can only govern a nation by tradition or by force. Until Parnell appeared on the scene, England was governed by tradition; after 1880 the Government began to be conducted by force, not the force of the sword, but of Parliamentary rules. "It is our business", said Burke, "so to be patriots as not to forget that we are gentlemen." It was an accident that seated one of the most finished gentlemen of his day in the Chair to assist in the change from the spirit of gentlemen to the spirit of violence. Let us consider for a moment the philosophy of procedure which underlies the technical jargon of the Standing Orders.

Walter Bagehot dealt a death-blow at the theory

of the British Constitution as evolved by the
philosophers and lawyers of the eighteenth century, Montesquieu, Blackstone and De Lolme.
The nicely adjusted system of checks and balances,
the deliberate division of power between Crown,
Lords and Commons, the separation of legislative,
judicial and executive functions, all this has been
recognised, ever since the appearance of Bagehot's
book in 1867, as mere theory, which fascinated
men of letters, and which misled Alexander
Hamilton into devising the worst Constitution the
world has ever seen. The British Constitution,
like every other living organism, is constantly
changing, and power is constantly being shifted
from one part of the Constitution to another, not
by deliberate compact, but merely as the result,
for the time being, of the battle. I remember many
years ago shocking the Treasury Bench by telling
its occupants that they were merely an Executive
Committee of the House of Commons. At least
two Ministers solemnly rebuked me by declaring
that they were the servants of the Crown, and
therefore not bound to supply the House with
information until it was too late to be of any
use. The servants of the Crown! So they are, in
the grave and respectful language of the pre-

Bagehotian theorists; in reality the Cabinet is a Committee of the two Houses of Parliament selected by the Prime Minister. It is the great merit of Herr Redlich[1] that, though a foreigner and a professor, he has not been imposed on by the pompous theories of the eighteenth century; but has grasped the very practical meaning of our quaint and courtly forms. During the eighteenth and the first half of the nineteenth century, the House of Commons was governed by custom and precedent, the *"lex et consuetudo Parliamenti"*, which were left to the Speaker and the clerks at the table to enounce. Speaker Onslow would tell Sir Robert Walpole or Mr. Pitt that the rule was so-and-so, and if the Chair was doubtful or disbelieved, an order would be made to search the Rolls of Parliament, or the Journals of the House, and to find a precedent. All this answered admirably so long as the House of Commons was what Professor Redlich calls "socially homogeneous", *i.e.* composed of English gentlemen of similar habits and education, not too much in

[1] Josef Redlich, *The Procedure of the House of Commons.* With an Introduction and Supplementary Chapter by Sir Courtenay Ilbert, K.C.S.I., Clerk to the House of Commons. 3 vols. London: Constable, 1908.

117

earnest, who recognised the Standing Orders as the rules according to which a pleasant and exciting game was to be played. The first transference of power from the upper to the middle class took place in 1832, and almost immediately a change was felt. "Before St. Stephen's Chapel was gutted by the fire of 1834 its occupants became aware of a difference in its atmosphere", writes Sir Courtenay Ilbert. "The keen wind of democracy had begun to whistle through the venerable and old-fashioned edifice." But the spirit of Eton and Oxford survived the first Reform Act for a considerable time, and it was not until forty-seven years later that "the observance of understandings" on which every Constitutional Government depends, was rudely abandoned by the Irish Nationalists. Parliamentary obstruction, like most other great inventions, was discovered by a man quite unknown to fame, one Ronayne, an Irish Nationalist member, who communicated his idea to its first and most celebrated practitioner, Joseph Biggar, an elderly provision merchant, of dwarfed and deformed figure, representing the county of Cavan. The story goes that Disraeli, coming in one day towards the third hour of one of Biggar's orations, fixedly regarded the apparition through his eyeglass. "George," he said at last to someone near him, "what is that thing?" "Oh, that's Biggar, the new member for Cavan." "Ah!" said Dizzy, in his deepest and most reflective tones, "I thought it had been a gnome sprung from the caverns of the earth." And Disraeli meant what he said, for he felt that he was confronted by a new and terrible power, and he almost immediately retired to the House of Lords. Parnell, who was elected in 1875, saw at a glance the genius of Ronayne's and Biggar's idea. Once recognise that all Parliamentary rules and conventions are, as Biggar said, "nonsense", and the opportunities of warfare are infinite. But it was not until the next Parliament, elected in 1880 with a Liberal majority, that both parties saw the necessity of making essential changes in the rules of business. Parnell and his style of fighting were at first regarded as a phenomenon that would pass as other Irish leaders and their methods had passed. But at length his energy and seriousness "shook the parties and their leaders out of their sleep. Their eyes were opened, and they saw obstruction in its true character as parliamentary anarchy, a revolutionary struggle, with barricades of speech on every highway and byway to the

Parliamentary market, hindering the free traffic which is indispensable for the conduct of business." As Mr. Timothy Healy said one night, "It is no longer a question of argument but of *avoir du pois*." Matters were brought to a head by Speaker Brand's *coup d'état* on January 31, 1881, when, after a sitting of forty-one hours, from 4 P.M. on Monday to 9 A.M. on Wednesday, he made a short and dignified speech to the House, and simply put the question. From that hour it was recognised that the rules of procedure, once a method of convenience, were become a weapon of warfare. From that day to this, successive Governments have done nothing but tamper with the rules of procedure, modifying or abolishing old rules, and passing new ones, until the Standing Orders of the House of Commons make quite a complicated chapter of technical knowledge. All the changes of procedure that were effected in 1881, in 1887, in 1896, in 1902 and in 1906, are set forth accurately in Professor Redlich's volumes, and brought up to date by the Clerk of the House of Commons. The details of these changes would hardly be intelligible, and certainly be uninteresting, to the average reader; while even for the scientific student of politics it is the moral significance of the rules, not the rules themselves, that matters. The three changes established by Mr. Gladstone, Mr. Balfour and the present Prime Minister are the Grand or Standing Committees (to take the place of Committees of the whole House), the closure and "the guillotine". The object of all these changes is to expedite, by curtailing discussion, an end which has been partially attained, but at the cost of almost everything that makes Parliamentary institutions valuable. Free and competent argument has gone by the board, and with it Parliamentary eloquence and independence of character. The power which the House of Commons has wrung, as the result of long struggles, first from the Crown, and then from the House of Lords, it has been compelled to surrender to the Cabinet. The Prime Minister of England is to-day more powerful than any Sovereign in the world, and far more powerful than the President of the United States, whose influence in the Legislature is extraneous and personal. The establishment of this ministerial oligarchy has not been the act of the people, still less the work of ambitious statesmen. It has been the unintended result of the action of an irreconcilable Parliamentary group, namely, the Irish

Nationalists. Verily the Irish have made us pay a heavy price for the Union. For in order to suppress the Irish we have been obliged to suppress ourselves. We have acted like the bear in La Fontaine's fable, who, taking up a rock to crush the fly upon the face of his sleeping friend, smashed his skull.

It must have been gall and wormwood to Speaker Peel to be obliged to watch and help such a change. Mr. Arthur Wellesley Peel (created a viscount in 1894) was a younger son of the second Sir Robert Peel, the Prime Minister, and had been a member of the House of Commons in the meridian of its fame and power. He had been Whip to the Liberal Party in the Palmerstonian era, and had witnessed the contests between Gladstone and Disraeli and Bright and Lowe—certainly the Augustan age of Parliament. Although he hardly ever spoke as a private member, or as a Government official, when Mr. Peel addressed the House from the Chair he discovered most of the qualities of the orator. A fine set of vocal chords seems to be hereditary in the family, for the third Sir Robert Peel had a beautiful voice, and that of the Speaker was rich, melodious and penetrating. His carriage was dignified; the few

gestures which he permitted himself were graceful: his choice of grave and vigorous language was
perfectly suited to the occasion. And this was the
man, steeped to the lips in the finest traditions of
the House of Commons, a fastidious student of
words and manners, whom fate selected to cope
with the calculated ruffianism of Parnell and his
band! No one could have succeeded as he did in
keeping order in those terrible days by sheer force
of character and manner. Even his fault of a quick
and arrogant temper, which did him so much dis-
service after he had entered the House of Lords,
served his purpose in the Chair, for Speaker Peel
was feared by the members as boys fear a strong
headmaster. I experienced this feeling myself
owing to an incident, which appears comical
enough to me now, but which at the time assumed
a tragic shape in my imagination. I was elected to
the House of Commons for the Peckham division
of Camberwell in November 1885. Almost immediately after the meeting of the new Parliament
in February 1886 Lord Salisbury's Government
was turned out by an amendment to the Address,
and Mr. Gladstone came in with his first Home
Rule Bill. The second-reading debate began in
April and lasted with intermissions for holidays

and necessary business, until June. The courteous custom of the House used to be that a new member, on rising for the first time, is called on by the Speaker before everybody else, and in those days even the Prime Minister or the Leader of Opposition would give way to a maiden orator. I prepared an elaborate and very excellent speech—much better than most of those that were delivered—against the Bill, and, counting on my privilege as a new member, went down night after night with my sheaf of notes. Unfortunately for me, the number of new members elected in 1885 was very large; and as I did not dare to stand up between 10 and 12 P.M., when the House is crammed with members in a state which Wendell Holmes describes as "the warm-champagny, brandy-punchy, old-particular feeling" and when they will listen to no one but the big guns, my chances were confined to the hours between 4 and 9 P.M. Weeks passed; my carefully pinned bundle of notes was beginning to wear thin and greasy: I did not mind that my arguments had been used, because I agree with Lord Chesterfield that in the House of Commons the subject-matter is common property; and it doesn't matter what you say, but how you say it. I thought that I could say what had already been said better than it had been said, and so I persevered. Once in my despair I thought of tearing up my notes, and preparing a speech in favour of the Bill, going to the Liberal Whip, making a splash and resigning my seat. But that temptation passed. It was one particularly dull evening (about the twelfth of my endurance), and I confided my sorrow to a friend sitting beside me, Colonel Arthur Brookfield, the member for Rye, and asked his opinion on my chance. "Stick to it", said Brookfield encouragingly, "he must call you in time." I sighed heavily, but even as I groaned a note was put into my hand, which I opened mechanically and therein read these words: "Dear Mr. Baumann—If you are ready to speak, I will call upon you next.—Yours truly, A. W. Peel". I showed the note to Brookfield, who said, "Exactly what I told you". Someone at the moment sat down, and I sprang confidently to my feet, but the Speaker called a gentleman on the other side of the House. By this time my tongue was parched, and I bethought me of what Disraeli calls "the juicy friendship of the fruit of Portugal", and slipped out to the bar in the Lobby. On my way back to my seat, whether inspired by some devil or merely emboldened by the wine, I stepped lightly on to the lower step of the throne (as I had seen older members do) and said quite casually, "I hope, Sir, that you will call on me next". The Speaker started, and threw up his head like a thoroughbred that has suddenly received a kick from the spiked heel. "Sir", said Peel, putting out his chin, as I have read his father used to do when annoyed, "I never make promises of that kind." "But, Sir," I replied in a puzzled way, "I have just received a letter from you saying that you would do so." "I never wrote such a letter in my life to any member of this House", whispered the Speaker in a voice now hoarse with fury; "show me the letter at once." I slunk back to my seat to find the letter which I had left in the little tray which runs along the back of the bench at one's knees, but the missive had disappeared! I searched on the seat, and in my hat, and under the seat, and felt all my pockets—no letter! I then turned to Brookfield and asked him whether I had given him the letter. "Letter? What letter? I suppose you mean this thing", and he thrust into my hand a piece of paper which I clutched triumphantly, and read these words: "Dear Mr. Baumann—If you are ready to speak I will call upon you next.—Yours truly, A. M.

Brookfield". I sat spellbound: the House began to swim before my eyes, when one of the Whips, leaning over the bench, said that the Speaker wished to speak to me. Like a man in a trance, with the cursed piece of paper in my hand, I made my way to the steps of the throne. "Well, Sir," said Peel, glaring at me, "have you got that letter?" "Yes, Sir, here it is." The Speaker put on his glasses, smoothed the piece of paper on his knee, and read it. "Well, Sir, this is not my letter: it is signed 'A. M. Brookfield'." "So I see now, Sir. I can only say that in my agitation I thought the signature was yours." This might have mollified the sternest despot; but Peel thought his dignity was affronted; and he waved me away with, "I shall consider whether I shall bring your conduct before the House". All this while the debate droned on, and the dinner hour was reached. Brookfield and I wandered up and down the lobbies, through the library and the smoking-room, discussing what we should do, and certainly I was the most miserable man in the House that night. Whilst we were perambulating, we descried in one of the lobbies the Right Hon. George Cavendish Bentinck. Here, we agreed, is the very man to advise us: a privy councillor, and one of the most experienced members of the House. We told our tale to the Right Hon. George, whose eyes twinkled as he listened, and we wound up by asking him tearfully what we should do. "Pooh! who the devil's Peel? Do? Why I should . . ."—and then the right hon. gentleman uttered one of those *grossièretés* which a lower-form public-school boy will use to describe what he would do to a tutor or master of whom he disapproves. Forcing a sycophantic smile to hide our horror, we fled. About ten o'clock Sir Michael Hicks Beach, who was then leading the Opposition, sent for us to his private room behind the Chair. The great man was calm, and easy, and smilingly invited us to tell him what we had been doing to upset the Speaker, who was in a terrible rage. When he had heard the story, Sir Michael's smile broadened into a grin, and he said, very sensibly, that the House of Commons was not the place for practical jokes; but that as the Speaker thought we meant to insult him, we must write letters of apology, which we accordingly did, and received an intimation from the Whips about midnight that "the incident was closed". It was only after I had despatched my apology that it flashed across me that Brookfield had, with great presence of mind, torn up the first letter and written the second letter, when he saw me talking to the Speaker on my return from the bar. The trick was so clever that, though it was played at my expense, I never could bring myself to be angry with Brookfield. But I told the facts to Mr. Walter Long and the Serjeant-at-Arms, Mr. Erskine, as he then was, meaning that they should reach the Speaker, as they did. Peel's method of making amends to me was characteristic of his fine and generous nature. From that time he treated me with the greatest courtesy and consideration. A week or so later I rose again—not in that infernal Home Rule Debate—and Sir William Harcourt for the Government rose at the same time. The Speaker called me, to Sir William Harcourt's rage and surprise, and that time I did succeed in making my maiden speech. I spoke again on another occasion, and the next night went to the Speaker's levee. The Speaker shook me warmly by the hand and said, "Allow me to congratulate you on your speech last night"; then, turning to the third Sir Robert Peel, who was standing beside him, he said, "Robert, let me introduce you to the member for Peckham, who made a very brilliant speech yesterday". I have always thought that Speaker Peel's methods of making amends to a young man whom he realised that he had treated harshly was one of the finest examples of good breeding I ever knew. But "other times, other manners". Perhaps Mr. Peel would not have done in the present House of Commons, whose members might think him too autocratic. Be that as it may, Arthur Peel was one of the greatest Speakers that ever sat in the Chair. Often in the silent watches of the night I act the tragedy of the duplicate letter over again, and see that angry face. *Admonet in somnis et turbida terret imago.*

XI

THE MARQUESS OF SALISBURY

THE MARQUESS OF SALISBURY

LORD SALISBURY'S life divides itself into three chapters. There was the period between 1853 and 1866, when Lord Robert Cecil was a younger son living with his wife and family on an allowance from his father and what he earned by writing articles in the *Quarterly* and *Saturday* Reviews. This was the bitter and rebellious period. There was the period between 1866 and 1881, when after the death of his brother and father, he bloomed into the marquisate, a large rent-roll, and the occupancy of Hatfield. During the last four years of this mellowing time he became Secretary for Foreign Affairs, and Lord Beaconsfield's first lieutenant. There was the final phase, from Disraeli's death in 1881 to his own death in 1903. He became leader of the Tory Party, and formed four Administrations, in '85, '86, '95 and 1900.

Lord Robert Cecil's boyhood and early youth are a dismal tale of ill-health and morbid egotism. He was bullied at school—as a boy will be who won't play games, who can't keep his hat on his head, or his clothes clean, and who gives no sign of intellectual precocity. He was obliged on the score of health to leave Christ Church after two years with what amounted to an honorary degree; and his beginning of life was a kind of hymn of hate. He hated his preparatory school; he hated Eton; he hated the Peerage and the Court Guide; and worst of all he hated Mr. Disraeli, fifteen years his senior, and the acknowledged leader of his party. What are we to say to a young man who, born in the purple, tells his father at the age of twenty-six: "I do not enjoy anything. Amusements I have none"? His father, who apparently wished to provide him with some occupation, offered him a colonelcy in the Middlesex Militia, to which Lord Robert replied, "Your proposition gave me a stomachache all this morning". Such morbidity is pathetic; but, although physically handicapped, he had no lack of moral courage. With £300 a year from his mother, and £100 a year from his father (not a very magnificent allowance from the Marquess of Salisbury to his son), Lord Robert Cecil married Miss Alderson with £100 a year of her own, and took a house in Fitzroy Square. In the middle of last century £500 a year was about the equivalent of £1000 to-day; but for a young Lord, born and bred at Hatfield, it was little enough wherewith to start married life. I doubt if Lord Robert ever made more than £300 or £400 a year by his pen. Four articles in the *Quarterly Review* would mean £160 by the tariff then ruling; he could not have made more than £200 a year out of the *Saturday Review*, even though it was run by his millionaire brother-in-law, Mr. James Beresford Hope, for the editor, J. D. Cook, did not always accept his articles, and sometimes kept them on hand for a longer time than a needy contributor likes. Putting all these things together, the Robert Cecils could not have had a larger income than £800 or £900; and one cannot help wondering what would have happened to the future Prime Minister if his elder brother had not died some ten years later.

In 1853 Lord Exeter popped Lord Robert Cecil in for Stamford, one of the small boroughs that escaped the scythe of the first Reform Act, and still remained in the pocket of a great family. For fifteen years Lord Robert was returned without a contest, which was really a misfortune; if he had been obliged to fight two or three contested elections he might have gained some knowledge of the character of *l'homme moyen sensuel*, who always was a perfect stranger to Lord Salisbury. During those fifteen years Lord Robert persistently and virulently attacked Disraeli in the *Saturday Review*, in the *Quarterly Review* and in *Bentley's Quarterly Review*. It was not surprising that Lord Exeter, who supplied the seat, and Lord Salisbury (the father), who paid the bills, should have remonstrated with this very independent member. Lord Robert Cecil's reply was that he voted with the party because by not doing so he might injure it —as if his writings in the Press did the party no injury! To Lord Exeter he explained more particularly that Disraeli was Lord Derby's lieutenant, and that it was the Derby Government that he supported. As Disraeli was leader of the party in the House of Commons, this was a very flimsy excuse. To his father, however, he gave another explanation. Disraeli was a personal friend of Lord Salisbury, who constantly received him at Hatfield, and who had accepted a post in the Tory Government of 1859. Naturally Lord Salisbury told his son that he objected not only to these anonymous attacks, but to the indecorous language in which they were couched. Lord Robert replied thus: "It must be remembered that I write for money . . . I must therefore write so as best to gain money. . . . What I do write I must write in a style that is most likely to attract, and therefore sell." And Lady Gwendolen harps on the cynicism of Lord Derby and Disraeli! I don't know how it may have been in the early Victorian era; but in the 'eighties, when I was in Parliament, and Lord Salisbury was Premier, a Conservative member who was known to attack his leader anonymously in the papers, and did so regularly for a livelihood, would have had a rough time in the lobbies and smoking-rooms. I should have thought there could be no two opinions about such conduct. The case is aggravated by the fact that Disraeli always went out of his way to be courteous and encouraging to the young member. Disraeli knew that his friend's son was persistently attacking him under the veil of anonymity, for Disraeli had been a journalist himself, and was perfectly informed as to what was going on in that world; yet in the Government formed by himself and Derby in 1866, Lord Cranborne, as the member for Stamford had become by the death of his brother, was offered and accepted the coveted post of Secretary of State for India. Such magnanimity is very rare in party politics, and might have placated its object. On the contrary, within a few months Lord Cranborne renewed his attacks upon the Leader of the House of Commons, both on the floor and in the Press, with increased venom. Now what are the facts about the Reform Bill of 1867? After the death of Lord Palmerston in 1866, Gladstone introduced a Reform Bill to lower the franchise in boroughs from £10 to £7 rental, and in the counties from £50 to £14. The Whigs thought the Bill went too far; the Radicals thought it did not go far enough; the Tories thought that it was the business of the Opposition to oppose. Between these forces Gladstone fell in the summer of 1866, and Lord Derby was invited by the Queen to form a Government in a Parliament with a hostile majority. Lord Derby might, of course, have dissolved; but besides the fact that there had been a General Election the year before, men of all parties, Whigs, Tories and Radicals, had time to reflect upon the situation. We had not yet got compulsory gratuitous education; but the artisans in the towns were beginning to educate themselves and their children by attendance at lectures and evening classes at the institutes. The writings of Darwin, Huxley and Tyndall were abroad, and permeating the mind of the nation. It really was impossible for any House of Com-

mons to postpone or trifle with the extension of
the franchise. Indeed, Lady Gwendolen herself, in
one of the happiest phrases of her book, explains
Disraeli's almost magical success in passing his
Reform Bill as "the avenging power of fact over
the self-created delusions of politicians". The first
person to perceive the realities of the situation was
Queen Victoria. After turning Gladstone out,
Disraeli was inclined to rest on his oars, while
Lord Derby was, as usual, only too delighted to
read racing results instead of Parliamentary de-
bates. But the Queen was a serious and resolute
woman; and she wrote a long letter to Lord Derby
insisting that his Government should settle without delay the question of Parliamentary reform.
This letter was written in October '66, and must
have been communicated to the November
Cabinet which Lord Cranborne attended. All
through December the discussion was continued
in the Cabinet, and it was decided to proceed by
tabling resolutions instead of introducing a Bill.
That was purely a question of method, not of
principle; and it was soon abandoned for a Bill.
This change was denounced by Lord Cranborne as
a species of political crime. The short time given
to drafting the clauses of the Bill was regarded by

General Peel, Lord Cranborne and Lord Carnarvon as political profligacy so dangerous that·they all resigned from the Cabinet at a peculiarly critical moment in February. General Peel one can forgive; he was avenging his brother. But what is to be said of Lords Cranborne and Carnarvon? The subject of Parliamentary reform had been steadily discussed for the past twenty years, and at least two Reform Bills had been introduced during Lord Cranborne's membership of the House of Commons. There was not a detail, not a clause, not a schedule, in any possible Reform Bill that was not perfectly familiar to every member on both sides of the House. Disraeli took his stand upon "the avenging power of fact" over party politics. He assumed as his major premiss, that, in the interest of the House of Commons as well as of the nation, the question of lowering the franchise had to be settled then and there, by and with the consent of all parties. Granting this assumption, in which the Sovereign and all his colleagues, with three exceptions, concurred, there was no question of principle involved; it was merely a matter of detail, of clauses and schedules. As the measure was to be passed with the co-operation of the whole House, it followed that the details had to be changed from time to time to secure acceptance by the different groups. Lady Gwendolen, with acid contempt, brands the policy as "pure opportunism". Of course it was; but opportunism is sometimes the highest wisdom. We shall find plenty of pure opportunism when we come to the Tory Governments of '85 and '86, and see Lord Carnarvon—who is exhibited to us in these pages as a Paladin of politics, the soul of honour and chivalry, shuddering at the pliability of Disraeli—as Viceroy of Ireland, twittering in the twilight of Parnellism.

When the Bill was passed, Lord Derby retired on the ground of ill-health, and Disraeli became Prime Minister in 1868. As the custom is, he was obliged to reconstruct his Government. With that absence of vindictiveness which marked his character, and which, I think, placed him on a higher moral plane than those who attacked him, Disraeli sent Sir Stafford Northcote to find out whether, now that the Reform question was out of the way, Lord Cranborne would rejoin the Cabinet. The answer was reported by himself in a letter to Lord Carnarvon: "I told him I had a great respect for every member of the Government except one— but that I did not think my honour was safe in the hands of that one". The wanton insolence and bad feeling of this reply can only be realised if we remember that the leading members of the Government were Cairns, Richmond, Stanley, Gathorne-Hardy and Stafford Northcote, who had all marched step by step with their Chief through the "Great Surrender". Lady Gwendolen surmises that "as Sir Stafford Northcote was eminently a man of peace", he did not transmit this message of his Chief. I should base my surmise on the fact that Sir Stafford Northcote was a gentleman.

In 1868, on his father's death, Lord Cranborne was translated from Duchess Street to Hatfield and Arlington Street, with a handsome rent-roll from London and Herts. Characteristically, the new Marquess of Salisbury opens a black suit. He groans over the burthen of estate management, and laments the boredom of hospitality. Nevertheless, the man was much improved by affluence and a peerage; he would have been more or less than human if he had not been. Lord Salisbury's temper, soured no doubt by early struggles with impecuniosity, was softened; his latent sense of humour was aroused; and something very like geniality took the place of austerity. After six years of Gladstone's plundering and blundering,

Disraeli found himself, for the first time in his
life, able to form a Government with a substantial
majority. It was impossible, even for Disraeli, to
forget the insult of 1868; and it was therefore
necessary to find an honest broker if Lord Salisbury was to join the Cabinet of 1874. The inter-
mediary appeared in the person of "My Lady",
Lord Salisbury's stepmother, then the wife of
Lord Derby, the "young Morose" of Disraeli's
early days. She succeeded in starting a correspondence between "My dear Lord" and "Dear
Mr. Disraeli", which ended in Lord Salisbury returning to the India Office. The relations between
the two men improved rapidly from that date,
although the confidence and admiration which the
older man extended to the younger were never
quite reciprocated. Indeed, in one of the letters
written by Lord Salisbury to his wife from the
Berlin Congress, it is rather amusing to find that
the Cecil family evidently regarded Lord Beaconsfield as a pottering figurehead, the success of the
business being, of course, due to his lieutenant.
On June 23, 1878, Lord Salisbury writes: "There
is no news since I wrote yesterday—except that
my Chief is distressing himself very much about
the supposed designs of Bismarck; what with deaf-

ness, ignorance of French, and Bismarck's extraordinary mode of speech, Beaconsfield has not the dimmest idea of what is going on—understands everything crossways—and imagines a perpetual conspiracy". I believe the second lion always thinks the first a bore.

"The greatest of British interests is peace", is a maxim only true if it be remembered that a nation may pay too high a price for peace. Lord Salisbury preserved peace in Europe whilst he lived. The question is whether his foreign policy did not lead inevitably to the Great War in 1914. The author of the saying just quoted was Lord Derby, who never said a foolish thing and seldom did a wise one. If his cold nature ever felt anything like affection and admiration for any public man it was for Lord Beaconsfield, who made him Foreign Secretary in the Cabinet of 1874. Yet he deserted his leader in 1878 because Lord Beaconsfield stopped Russia at the gates of Constantinople by despatching the Fleet to the Dardanelles and calling Indian troops to Malta. Lord Salisbury had at last recognised the commanding personality which he had so long resisted. He succeeded Lord Derby at the Foreign Office, and "the master of flouts and gibes" had no words too strong to condemn the impotent pacifism of his late colleague.

He compared Lord Derby's explanation to the discoveries of Titus Oates, and summed up his character in one of the wittiest and bitterest epigrams in the range of political invective. "My noble friend", he said, "will never stray far from the frontier lines of either party, and he reserves all his powers of being disagreeable for those with whom he is temporarily associated." The action from which Lord Derby shrank, with the flawless logic of a pacifist, forced Russia to submit the treaty which had been wrung from Turkey at San Stefano to the arbitrament of the European Powers, who saved Constantinople by the Treaty of Berlin. Would that Lord Salisbury had adhered to the Eastern policy of Disraeli! No sooner had the election of 1880 removed Lord Beaconsfield from power than Gladstone began the reversal of his rival's foreign policy. Indeed, he could hardly avoid doing so, seeing that the Bulgarian atrocities campaign of 1877 and the Midlothian campaign of 1880 consisted of nothing but denunciations of the "unspeakable Turk" and the Minister who had protected him. At the opening of Parliament in 1881 Lord Beaconsfield complained that, in defiance of the tradition of continuity policy, the new Government had given the order for "per-petual and complete reversal of all that had occurred" in foreign, Colonial and Irish affairs. That the Liberal Party should have so acted was bad enough; but that Lord Salisbury should have been induced to abandon Lord Beaconsfield's policy of supporting the Sultan for the policy, partly religious, partly philanthropic and wholly sentimental, of patronising the Balkan States, was deplorable; and exactly the consequences pre-dicted by Lord Beaconsfield ensued in the follow-ing thirty years. Lord Beaconsfield's policy of maintaining the independence and territorial in-tegrity of Turkey was no sentimental predilection of a Jew for his cousins of the Koran; it was a clear perception of the realities of world politics, supplemented by a profound knowledge of human nature. In July 1878, Lords Beaconsfield and Salisbury returned from Berlin and drove in triumph from Charing Cross to Downing Street, bringing peace with honour. A few days later the Prime Minister expounded his Eastern policy to a crowded House of Lords. "Her Majesty's Govern-ment at all times have resisted the partition of Turkey", said Lord Beaconsfield. "They have done so because, apart from the high moral considerations that are mixed up with the subject, they believed an attempt on a great scale to accomplish the partition of Turkey would inevitably lead to a long, a sanguinary, and often recurring struggle, and that Europe and Asia would both be involved in a series of troubles and sources of disaster and danger of which no adequate idea could be formed." We know now the troubles, disasters and dangers in which Europe and Asia have been involved by the attempt to partition Turkey.

The ancients, with true philosophic instinct, refused to pronounce any man happy until he was dead. Lord Salisbury ended a great and busy life more happily, it seems to me, than any of his predecessors, except Lord Palmerston. He alone, true to the Ha! Ha! style until his death, passed peacefully away in actual possession of the symbols of authority if not of governing power. When Lord Salisbury retired in 1902 he was the benevolent despot of a united party, which was more powerful in Parliament and in the constituencies than any British party had ever been before. He enjoyed in unstinted measure the confidence of his Sovereign; and he was, unquestionably, the most influential statesman in the world. What more could the heart of man desire? There is something more which the heart of every good man desires, and that was given to Lord Salisbury. He saw the growing success of those who were near to him, whom he wished to please, and whom he loved. His eldest son (Lord Cranborne) was Under-Secretary of State for Foreign Affairs. Another of his sons (Lord Hugh Cecil) was acknowledged to be amongst the most brilliant orators in the House of Commons. Another (Lord Edward) had distinguished himself as an officer in the South African War; while yet another (Lord Robert) was enjoying a lucrative practice at the Parliamentary bar. One of his daughters was married to a young statesman (Lord Selborne) of blameless reputation and occupant of the post of First Lord of the Admiralty. One of his nephews was First Lord of the Treasury (Mr. Arthur Balfour), Leader of the House of Commons and his uncle's inevitable successor. Another nephew (Mr. Gerald Balfour) was President of the Board of Trade, and a sister's daughter was married to the Chairman of Ways and Means (Mr. J. W. Lowther). Surely no statesman was ever so happy in his public and private life as Lord Salisbury.

It is remarkable that Lord Salisbury never really

had a rival, in the sense of a contemporary competitor for power, either on his own side or the opposite. Gladstone and Disraeli, who were much of an age, were his seniors by about fifteen years, and belonged to a previous generation. Nevertheless, Lord Salisbury made more than one attempt to overthrow the adventurous genius, whom he secretly disliked with the *morgue* of a great English noble. But Disraeli was too much for him, and during the lifetime of that dominating personality, Lord Salisbury was obliged to play second fiddle. Competitors for the first place he had none, for the Gathorne-Hardys and Stafford Northcotes belonged to a different category of men. The fifteenth Lord Derby at one time threatened him as a possible successor to Disraeli; but Lord Derby was cursed with the judicial mind; and his retirement from Lord Beaconsfield's Ministry in 1878, upon the calling out of the reserves, and his subsequent acceptance of office from Mr. Gladstone, made Lord Salisbury's succession secure. When Lord Beaconsfield died, Lord Salisbury found himself confronted for a short time by Mr. Gladstone, who had enjoyed in the country a power immeasurably greater than his own. It is more than doubtful whether Lord Salisbury could have defeated Home Rule without the assistance of Lord Hartington and Mr. Chamberlain. However, that assistance he obtained, and on the ruins of the Liberal Party he rose to the ascendancy in his own country and the outer world which he claimed and kept from 1886 until 1902.

On Mr. Gladstone's retirement in 1894, Lord Salisbury's position can only be compared to that of the second Pitt; he was on a pedestal apart; there was no one near him. To Lord Kimberley, the titular leader of the House of Lords, he extended the grave courtesy due to official position and respectability. Lord Rosebery he always treated as the spoilt and brilliant boy whose exuberant declamation was to be smiled at rather than answered. It was a misfortune for Lord Salisbury that he was not confronted by a rival of his own age, by a foeman worthy of his steel. Every man requires a whetstone, and latterly Lord Salisbury became sluggish, and too indifferent to the man in the street.

How did Lord Salisbury achieve the position of one of the most powerful Premiers that ever ruled the British Empire? By the old, though always rare, qualities of industry, courage and rectitude of character. He had high rank and considerable wealth, which helped him much. What would have become of Lord Robert Cecil had his elder brother lived, it is idle to speculate. But other Prime Ministers have had rank and wealth. Lord Rockingham and the Duke of Portland, for instance, who had passed quickly across the stage leaving no memory behind them. It was not his marquisate, or his rent-roll, that gave Lord Salisbury his power over his countrymen and Europe. Lord Salisbury won his place by much the same virtues as other men have used to raise themselves from humble positions. He was an indefatigable worker, sitting at his desk, it is said, for thirteen out of the twenty-four hours.

Whether he was constitutionally incapable of remembering a manuscript or whether he thought that the result was not worth the labour, I do not know, but the habit of not even writing notes beforehand prevented Lord Salisbury's speeches from ranking as oratory. For though the style was incisive and correct, generally humorous and sometimes witty, it was too disjointed and familiar to be read in print by posterity. Indeed Lord Salisbury despised rhetoric, just as he despised self-advertisement, and sham philanthropy, and the other demagogic arts. Sometimes his simplicity was very dramatic. Addressing a huge meeting of working men in a South London music-hall, the Prime Minister wiped his brow with the back of his hand. The familiar gesture at once put an audience of shy artisans at their ease. He dealt with the Balkan question. "I have in my pocket", said Lord Salisbury, "a letter from the Sultan of Turkey, which I will read to you", and, fumbling in the breast pocket of his frock-coat, he pulled out a bundle of letters, from which he selected one, and said, "The Sultan asks me to tell the people of England", and then began to read a few words about Turkish reform probably dictated by the British Ambassador at Constantinople. The artisans, clerks and dock labourers gasped with excitement. Here was a man who walked about with letters from the crowned heads of Europe jumbled up with his ordinary correspondence! And this man was standing there talking to them! This was something like politics!

At other times his simplicity had the effect of an Olympian rebuke. During one of the violent phases of the Irish question between '85 and '92 some credulous Radical wrote to Lord Salisbury asking whether it was true, as reported in the papers, that he had signed a treaty with Mr.

Parnell in the smoking-room of the House of Commons, to which the following reply was sent: "Sir, Lord Salisbury desires me to say (1) he has never seen Mr. Parnell; (2) he has never been in the smoking-room of the House of Commons. I am, Sir, yours faithfully", etc.

This contempt for popularity was, of course, one of the sources of his power over the democracy. It must, however, be admitted that, in what may be called the lyrical power of statesmen, the power of saying in great language what the nation is thinking, Lord Salisbury was exasperatingly deficient. It was not that he failed to "read their history in a nation's eyes"; no man saw further or more clearly ahead than Lord Salisbury; but he scorned to avail himself of what Burke called "swelling sentiments" for the purpose of encouragement or consolation. At the beginning of the Boer War, for instance, when everybody was in despair at our reverses, and when the nation was thirsting for a patriotic speech, the Prime Minister stolidly declined to be dithyrambic, and persisted in treating Colenso as a twopenny-halfpenny Somaliland affair. It is very likely that this apparent apathy and levity concealed a deep policy with regard to foreign nations; but at the time it was chilling and disappointing. Partly, I think, it was due to his health, which ebbed with the century. I heard him make one of his last speeches in the House of Lords in which he warned the nation against overtaxing its strength by a policy of military adventure. But the drowsiness of delivery made me sad, as I knew the end could not be far off.

The austerity of Lord Salisbury's habits was another factor which contributed to his influence. Nothing impresses the masses more than the spectacle of a man, who might gratify all the senses of the voluptuary, living simply, and devoting himself to the public service. He never smoked, for even the fumes of a cigarette gave him a headache. He ate heartily, like all men who use their brains hard, but to the pleasures of the table in the epicurean sense he was a stranger. He was conspicuously careless in his dress, and he was not interested in his carriages and horses. In his old age he was seen riding a tricycle down to the Foreign Office with flying coat-tails and a soft black hat. He neither hunted nor shot, though on rare occasions he carried a gun about the park at Hatfield in company with his boys. When people said that Lord Salisbury was a cynic they meant that he did not believe in legislation as a cure for social ills. They could not mean it in any other sense. For he was a religious man, attached to the Church, and with strong family affections, as I have already observed. Though his pride and shyness prevented him from mixing easily with his fellows, and though most of his supporters in the House of Commons and some of his colleagues outside the Cabinet were unknown to him by sight, his nature was so generous that he was sometimes imposed upon by importunity and impudence. Once you had gained access to him, Lord Salisbury's courtesy was exquisite, and he assumed the soothing manner of a family physician. In legislation he assuredly did not believe, and it is not therefore as a lawmaker that he will fill his niche in history. The Bill for the creation of Parish Councils had been advocated on the ground that it would amuse the rural population. "I deny", said Lord Salisbury, "that it is the duty of the Government to provide amusement for the people. But if that be any part of its function, I should suggest a circus."

Lord Salisbury's reputation will rest on the following achievements. He defeated, and actually killed, the Home Rule that would have subjected

North-East Ulster to the government of the Celtic South and West Ireland; he kept the peace between Britain and the United States when President Cleveland sent his insulting message respecting Venezuela, and between Britain and France when Colonel Marchand was minded to hoist the tricolour at Fashoda; he stopped the European Powers from helping Spain in its quarrel with the United States over Cuba; and he prevented the intervention of the European Powers in our South African War. The two latter diplomatic victories he won by clearly explaining that whoever fought against the Americans or with the Boers would have to fight England. And Europe shut up like a telescope at the sight of Lord Salisbury's teeth.

In each of these great triumphs of statesmanship may be detected the ground-note of his character and career. Lord Salisbury was not an orator; nor a party manager; nor a propounder of programmes. But he was one of the greatest Prime Ministers of the last century, because he had the power of sobriety, the quality which the Greeks called σωφροσύνη, the sane and fearless mind, working without friction in its proper plane.

XII

LORD CHESTERFIELD

XII

LORD CHESTERFIELD

LORD CHESTERFIELD has suffered the rare misfortune of being tried and sentenced by his particular enemy. For one person who has read his *Letters* ten have read Boswell; and so it happens that the majority think of Lord Chesterfield as a feeble and immoral fop, who tried to teach his son how to dance a minuet and seduce a woman. Nothing could be farther from the truth. Like all classical work, the value of the *Letters* is not impaired by the lapse of time; for though we no longer wear silk coats and make low bows, the essentials of good manners are, and must always remain, the same. Far astray indeed was the editor of Chesterfield who laid down in his preface that "we have clearly no right to regard the *Letters* as a kind of 'Popular Educator'." That is just what they are, an up-to-date manual, never more needed than at present, when success is admitted to be the object of us all. To those who reject the gospel of getting-on, the *Letters* will of course be useless, if not repugnant. But Lord Chesterfield was haunted by no doubts of the truth of his gospel. He was intensely practical, and fortune had placed him in a position to take a near and leisurely view of many phases of life. He had been in the House of Commons and in the diplomatic service; he had been a Cabinet Minister and Viceroy of Ireland. As the result of unbiassed observation—for serenity and impartiality were the notes of Lord Chesterfield's mind—he came to the conclusion that for success in life there is nothing so important as a good manner. It requires a rare degree of mental clearness and independence to reach and state this conclusion, so contrary to the popular maxims about industry, will and the rest. Our success or failure in the world depends upon what we get, or fail to get, from others who will always rather give to one who is agreeable than to one who is disagreeable. What a truism this seems, and yet how few young men realise it! Dr. Johnson, notwithstanding his ferocious epigram, had occasional glimpses of the truth of his enemy's philosophy, for the difference between a well-bred and an ill-bred man, he observes, is this: "One immediately attracts your liking, and the other your aversion. You love the one until you find reason to hate him; you hate the other till you find reason to love him."

But if good manners be, as few will deny, so important for success in life, how comes it that it is the one part of our education that is left to take care of itself? Games and books are regarded as essential, and the progress of the child in one or the other, or both, according to the taste of the parent, is anxiously watched. But most parents and all young persons would receive with amused contempt or fierce resentment the idea that the habit of being agreeable to others is very useful, and can be taught. And here it is worth noticing the difference between the English and the French view of good breeding. When an Englishman uses the term "well-bred", he refers to the person's pedigree. "He was not bred in our kennel", said a Whig peer with coarse contempt of Mr. Gladstone. But the equivalent phrase in French, *bien élevé*, refers to the person's upbringing or education. The majority of English men and women regard good breeding as a thing which cannot be taught, but is partly congenital, and partly inhaled unconsciously from our social atmosphere. Lord Chesterfield took emphatically the French view, and his failure to teach his son good manners does not prove that the system was wrong, but merely that the son was deficient in intelligence. "Good breeding is the natural result of common sense and common observation. Common sense points to civility, and observation teaches you the manner of it, which makes it good breeding." There is nothing of the stud-book about this definition of breeding, which is again enforced in the following striking way. "Observe carefully what pleases you in others, and probably the same thing in you will please others. If you are pleased with the complaisance and attention of others to your humours, your tastes, or your weaknesses, depend upon it the same complaisance and attention on your part to theirs will equally please them." This of course is the secret of the business. Good manners consist in consideration for other people, that is to say, in intelligent altruism in small matters. It is absurd to say that this kind of unselfishness in trifles cannot be cultivated, because it is largely a matter of attention. Chesterfield complains bitterly of those old people who remain children in knowledge of the world to the end through their "levity and inattention". For the form of ill breeding which is known as absent-mindedness he had no mercy; and indeed there is no kind of rudeness which is more offensive than that of not listening to what is said to you because you are thinking of something else. "When you are reading Puffendorf, do not think of Madame de St. Germain, nor of Puffendorf when you are talking to Madame de St. Germain." How much more supportable life would be if the lady whom one took in to dinner gave her steady and un-dissipated attention to what was said to her for a brief hour, instead of looking round the table to make notes on other ladies' dresses, or trying to catch what her neighbours were saying to one another! "It is the sure answer of a fool, when you ask him about anything that was said or done when he was present, that 'truly he did not mind it'. And why did not the fool mind it? What else had he to do there, but to mind what was doing?"

There is another very common form of ill breed-ing which this great master of worldly science condemns with equal severity, that, namely, of not learning correctly the names or titles of others, and miscalling or mispronouncing them. There is no more certain sign of good breeding (using the term in the French sense) than this precision about names. Well-bred people are at pains to find out all about their company, if they are going amongst strangers. The rude and underbred will not take the trouble, or think it does not matter.

So that it all comes round to Chesterfield's saying that good manners are mainly a matter of taking pains, of paying attention, of concentrating one's mind upon the business of the moment.

The question is still unanswered whether the manners of the young should be left to chance, or should form part of their education. The truth, as usual, lies between the extremes, between the English view that manners are congenital or, as Chaucer puts it, that

Gentilesse cometh from God alone,

and the French Chesterfieldian view that good breeding does not depend upon birth or temperament, but upon training. Manners we take it are an affair of imitation, and it is the vulgarest error to suppose that mimicry is a low or animal art, for its successful practice demands a keen eye, a delicate ear and a retentive memory. In the early stages of life the child unconsciously imitates the speech and gestures of those around, and this is the only argument in favour of the English theory of breeding, for the child who is surrounded by the best models will naturally have the best manners. But in the later, conscious period, "common sense and common observation" will tell, for the son of the peer and the merchant or professional man will go through exactly the same education. An alert observation of details, and a sleepless perception of self-interest, have far more to do with good manners than benevolence or an inherited aptitude. Success has an extraordinary effect in mending or mellowing the manners, and I have known adventurers (in the good sense of the term), who before their success were churlish and awkward, expand into the most genial and polished of mortals after they had won money and fame. But the point I am labouring to establish is that manners are to a high degree teachable, and that parents can do a very great deal to make their children agreeable by impressing upon them the worldly utility of being so, for no other argument would be of the least avail. It is much to be wished that parents would do so, for the manners of the rising generation are marked by unabashed selfishness and cynical irreverence. The type of well-bred youth or maiden is, if not obsolete, rapidly obsolescent. Formerly there were well-recognised railings between the different ages; but, encouraged by their parents, the modern youths have incontinently stormed these barriers and are everywhere at all times. I have seen young ladies refuse to leave the dinner-table with their mother, and remain to romp with boys upon the hearthrug, to the dismay of the men, who, with sickly smiles of counterfeited glee, tried to sip their port and talk their politics. I have seen young gentlemen with turned-up trousers and the perennial cigarette between their lips lounge away the afternoon in their mother's drawing-room, staring silently at her guests through rings of smoke. It is impossible that young people so brought up can be other than selfish and inconsiderate men and women. So long as they are young, they may get their way, for we are criminally indulgent to mere nonage. So long as they can buy what they want, it may be well with them. But should they have to enter the race as competitors, they will bitterly regret the fondness of their parents in not teaching them to do unto others as they would be done by. If they have brains they will correct their bad education, for when all has been said, bad manners are due to a defect of intelligence.

XIII

AN IRISH TRIUMVIRATE

XIII

AN IRISH TRIUMVIRATE

THE sudden and sinister turn which we have seen take place in the politics of the Irish Free State reminds us how completely the Irishman has vanished from the national life of Britain. It is not only that Irish politicians have ceased from troubling the House of Commons, but that Sandy has played Paddy off the music-hall and dramatic stage; that the fountain of English wit plays kindly upon the penuriousness of the former instead of the recklessness of the latter; and that both in literature and polite society Mr. Bernard Shaw remains the sole survivor of a joyous tradition. Ever since the beginning of the century Ireland's ineffectual fire has paled; and Colonel Saunderson and Oscar Wilde (may the colonel forgive the conjunction!) were the last witty Irishmen of my recollection.

The eighteenth century is the century of exclusiveness, of rhetoric, of wit polished and patronised by the aristocracy. Politics were monopolised by the great Whig and Tory families, who were shrewd enough to relinquish outside Parliament all claim to intellectual dominion.

Outside the Court and Parliament the intellectual world of London during the latter half of the century was ruled by half a dozen men: Johnson, Reynolds, Garrick, Goldsmith, Burke and Sheridan. The last three were Irish adventurers, whose wit was their only weapon, and who resembled one another by their perpetual willingness to borrow money to cure their chronic impecuniosity.

Of the triumvirate Oliver Goldsmith was the eldest; he was a year older than Burke, and the most unfortunate. He never emerged from the trough of the sea, those thirty years of stagnation which followed the Queen Anne period, and the deaths of Swift, Pope and Bolingbroke, when literature was chilled by a boorish and ignorant foreigner on the throne. Had he lived a few years longer I believe the author of *The Vicar of Wakefield* and *She Stoops to Conquer* would have mounted on the wave-crest that bore Burke to such meridian heights of fame. As it was, he died at forty-six, from sheer want and worry. Apart from the silliness and sentimentality of the story, I regard *The Vicar of Wakefield* as the purest piece of prose in the language.

But Goldsmith was not the mere sentimentalist: he was on occasion as much a master of that hard verbal felicity, the peculiar quality of Irish wit, as Sheridan or Wilde. "The Irish are a fair people, sir", said Johnson, "they never speak well of each other." Certainly Goldsmith's lines in *Retaliation* on Burke are as biting a commentary on his great friend's failures as anything Hazlitt ever penned. When you have said of a Parliament man that "he went on refining while they thought of dining", and that

'Twas his fate, unemploy'd or in place, sir,
To eat mutton cold and cut blocks with a razor,

you have uttered a criticism which in these days would be described as devastating.

The most splendid rhetorician and the profoundest political philosopher that ever lived was sandwiched between the awkward, unlucky Oliver and the meteoric Dick. Burke died in 1797, just as the Sheridan star was rising. Unless we realise how small was the political world in the eighteenth century, we shall be puzzled by the sudden leap into eminence of Burke.

He came to London about the same time as Goldsmith, just the middle of the century, and only a little less poor. Like Disraeli, he fastened at once on to "the great game" by writing not political novels, but a clever skit on Bolingbroke, *A Vindication of Natural Society*. For ten years he hung loose upon the town, writing Dodsley's *Annual Register*, then went back to Ireland as Single-Speech Hamilton's private secretary, and in 1765 found himself secretary to the Marquess of Rockingham, the chief of one of the three or four Whig gangs who put one another in and out of office, and Member for Wendover by the grace of Lord Verney. The Rockingham Ministry lasted only one year, but found time to repeal Grenville's Stamp Act, which was re-enacted by their successors.

Burke made his maiden speech as soon as he had taken his seat, and his extraordinary knowledge and ability were at once recognised by friends and foes. For the thirty years that followed Burke was the Whig party. He was their organiser, their orator and their pamphleteer. Yet he was only in office for nine months, and then in the subordinate place of Paymaster-General! We all know what he wrote, beginning with the *Thoughts on the Present Discontents*, and ending with the *Letters on a Regicide Peace*. His speeches on the

172

American War are classical, though they were delivered to half-empty benches, and disturbed by the noise of nut-cracking and sucking oranges.

Burke was too long, his voice was harsh, and he had a brogue that might be cut with a knife. He led the impeachment of Warren Hastings, and he gathered together the force of his dying years for a final spring upon the French Revolution. The last flame of the fire was, to my mind, the strongest and brightest, but perhaps that is because I hate the Bolshevists of the eighteenth as much as those of the twentieth century.

His end in his sixty-seventh year was pathetic. He did not mind his debts, any more than Dizzy. But his son, a fatuous youth whom he idolised, had died, and he saw that Pitt was so mishandling the war as to offer peace to the Terrorists. He is described as lounging over the dinner-table, with unbuttoned shirt-sleeves and disordered dress, trying to smile languidly at the pleasantries of Mrs. Crew, who, with Arthur Young and Windham and his wife, strove to soothe his last hours.

We know more of Sheridan than of the other two members of the triumvirate, partly because he lived nearer to our own day, and partly because his life had more facets than Burke's.

Sheridan touched the pageantry of life at many points. He was manager of Drury Lane, playwright, orator in Parliament and man of fashion, being, until the last few years, book companion and political adviser of the Prince of Wales. He was also a leading figure in the Devonshire House set, where Lady Ponsonby has written terrible things about him. Sheridan no doubt was told of Lady Ponsonby's accusations, and consoled himself with one of the best of his own apothegms: "When a scandalous story is believed against you, there is no consolation like the consciousness that it is deserved".

Byron said that "whatever Sheridan has done or chosen to do has been *par excellence* the best of its kind. He has written the best comedy (*School for Scandal*), the best farce (*The Critic*), and, to crown all, delivered the very best oration (the Begum's speech) ever conceived or heard in this country." When this was repeated to Sheridan he burst into tears. When somebody told him that the historian was delighted with "the luminous page of Gibbon" in the Westminster Hall speech, "Sure, I said voluminous", was Sheridan's correction.

He was indeed deadly in debate. "There is

much that is new and much that is true in the hon. member's speech. Unfortunately, sir, what is new is not true, and what is true is not new." Lord Belgrave, the son of Lord Westminster, ended his maiden speech by a quotation from Demosthenes in the original. Indulgence for the boy and respect for his rank, then a reality, produced a dead silence, which Sheridan thus broke, in a House composed of members who were all familiar with Homeric tags: "*Ton d' apameibomenos prosephe Sheridanius heros.*" One can imagine the shouts of laughter.

Sheridan's end, the fall from splendour to disgrace, was perhaps sadder than those of his two compatriots. Let us reflect what we owe to the genius of these three Irishmen. We cannot, if we would, forget the rich inexhaustible legacy they have left to us and to coming generations. It is one of the gravest charges against modern democracy that it has smothered with the blanket of its dull and sour disputations, the grace and gaiety of the Irish spirit.

XIV

ANTHONY TROLLOPE

XIV

ANTHONY TROLLOPE

IT says little for the taste of the last quarter of
the Victorian age that Anthony Trollope's autobiography, published in 1883 by his son Henry,
should have been for many years ignored or
derided. A publisher, more foolish than most,
exclaimed that the autobiography had killed the
remnant of Trollope's reputation.

It is now recognised that the little book is the
best literary life of the nineteenth century, if we
except Trevelyan's *Macaulay*. It has the candour
of Pepys, without his diffuseness and indecent
familiarity. It has the brevity of Gibbon, without
the stateliness of the great historian. Trollope was
no hero to himself. He doesn't bore you with his
pedigree or the cradle of his race, as so many men
of good family, when they sit down to write their
story, are prone to do. He tells you that the two
objects of his life were to be Anthony Trollope—
"digito monstrari et diceri: Hic est"—and to make
enough money to enjoy himself and provide for his
family.

It will not, I trust, be supposed that I have intended in this so-called autobiography to give a record of my inner life. No man ever did so truly—and no man ever will. If the rustle of a woman's petticoat has ever stirred my blood; if a cup of wine has been a joy to me; if I have thought tobacco at midnight in pleasant company to be one of the elements of an earthly paradise; if now and again I have somewhat recklessly fluttered a five-pound note over a card-table—of what matter is that to any reader? I have betrayed no woman. Wine has brought me to no sorrow. It has been the companionship of smoking that I have loved, rather than the habit. I have never desired to win money, and I have lost none. To enjoy the excitement of pleasure, but to be free from its vice and ill-effects —to have the sweet and leave the bitter untasted— that has been my study. The preachers tell us that this is impossible. It seems to me that hitherto I have succeeded fairly well. I will not say that I have never scorched a finger—but I carry no ugly wounds.

Trollope never made any pretence of religion, and to his nature mysticism was impossible. But if there be a better defence of apolaustic life I do not know it.

What offended or made people laugh in the autobiography was the revelation of the great novelist's methods of writing. Awakened by his groom, Trollope sat down to his desk every morning at 5 (or was it 4.30?) and, with his watch before him, wrote 250 words per fifteen minutes for three hours, when he breakfasted, and either rode on an indifferent hunter to the nearest meet or set about his duty as a Post Office inspector. He had a pad or block on which he wrote in crowded railway carriages, and a desk fixed up in his cabin when he was at sea.

It is impossible not to smile when he tells us that as he was writing that charming story of love and fox-hunting in *Framley Parsonage* he had frequently to leave a chapter unfinished on the saloon table and retire to his cabin to be sick. But if we laugh we must also admire the triumph of mind over matter. Only the ignorant could be disturbed by the steady tale of bricks in the small hours of the morning.

The ways of every art are tedious. Do we know how many times Millais or Sargent painted out the arm of a beauty? Or how many hours Tennyson or Swinburne spent over their stanzas? Trollope, a little perversely, pours scorn on the inspiration of art, and insists a trifle too much that the making of books is a trade, like the making of any other article in which success is only and always attainable by steady and punctual industry.

In the course of thirty years, between 1853 and his death in 1882, Trollope published some fifty books, of which forty-seven were novels, nearly all in three volumes, and he made about £75,000. One habit he had which he shared with Henry James. The morning after he had finished a novel he began another. He boasts of having written more than Carlyle and as much as Voltaire. To have been the most prolific writer of his day, and at the same time an efficient servant of the Post Office, is something of which a man in his closing years may fairly be proud.

The Warden was the first of the Barsetshire series and the foundation of Trollope's fortune, though at the time of its publication, and for three years after, he received from his publisher £19. In later years he derived a comfortable income from it as one of the group. "In the course of the job I visited Salisbury, and whilst wandering there one midsummer evening round the purlieus of the Cathedral, I conceived the story of *The Warden*." A wag, who was himself a high official in the Post Office, explained Trollope's extraordinary insight into the life of the Close and clerical character by declaring that the inspector opened the letters of the Bishop and Dean and Chapter.

Trollope, who would have died rather than own an imagination, assures us that he evolved the Barchester dignitaries out of his "moral consciousness". He drew what he thought an archdeacon should or would be, and Archbishop Grantly stood out, clear-cut and lifelike. The Bishop and Mrs. Proudie are perhaps the highest reach of Trollope's portraiture in the clerical line. The great masters of characterisation—Thackeray, Balzac, Carlyle, Macaulay—took pains to get their scenery right. Carlyle visited Germany, and Macaulay Ireland and the Midlands, with this object. Trollope took no such trouble, and though he learned the ritual life of the Cathedral, and discoursed about precentors and rural deans correctly enough, he got into a mess when he took to describing lawyers and politicians.

Whatever he wrote about the Civil Service—in Sir Raffle Buffles he got back a bit of his own on Maberley and Rowland Hill—or about fox-hunting, was first-hand knowledge. But he knew less about the procedure of the law than most laymen, certainly less than the son of a barrister ought to know. No novelist or dramatist need introduce a trial at bar; but if he does, he should get it right, or he spoils his effect. The trial of

Lady Mason in *Orley Farm* is a tissue of absurdities and blunders, which Sir Francis Newbolt has ruthlessly exposed. Nevertheless, the character of Furnival, the elderly and eloquent common law counsel, who is brought down "special", though he is only a "stuff", to defend Lady Mason, with whom he is in love, is well done, that is to say, as to his senile philandering and his crossness to his wife. Chaffenbrass, too, is a good caricature of the Old Bailey barrister as he was, though he does have chambers in Ely-place! In the whole range of his novels Trollope is only really successful with one lawyer, both as to character and to setting.

It is a striking instance of how an author may misjudge his works that Trollope should declare *Ralph the Heir* to be the worst of his novels, and to have clean forgotten Sir Thomas Underwood, ex-Solicitor-General and defeated candidate for Percy-cross. Unhesitatingly I give my opinion that *Ralph the Heir* is one of the best of the novels, and that Sir Thomas Underwood, as a retired leader of the Bar, excusing his idleness by a *magnum opus* on Francis Bacon, of which he never wrote a line, is one of the greatest creations in fiction.

Trollope's politics are sad trash, though again,

as with lawyers, the characterisation of the minor persons is masterly. What sticks are Mr. Gresham (Gladstone) and Mr. Daubigny (Disraeli)! Was there ever a more futile and impossible hero than Phineas Finn? A penniless Irish adventurer, who says little or nothing, but who, his creator tells us, is good-looking and pleasant, especially to women, is easily promoted to Ministerial rank and married to a wealthy and fashionable widow, when all the time there is no reason for his existence. All our novelists have tried their hand at the English gentleman, and all have failed. Fielding's Allworthy is too good; Dickens has given us Sir Leicester Dedlock, a purely fanciful sketch. Colonel Newcome, for all his Don Quixote manners, carries his foolishness in money matters to the point of criminality. Mr. Brooke of Tipton is a rambling old boy whose discursiveness and indolence allow Dorothea to marry Casaubon.

Trollope tells us that if Plantagenet Palliser, Duke of Omnium, was not a great English gentleman, then he knew not the meaning of the term. Planty Pal as a member of society is a prig; as a politician he is a poop; as husband and father he is pompous and unsympathetic. All my sympathy is with Lady Glencora, whom Trollope puts down as vulgar, but whom I love, if her manners do give a little in the heroine of musical comedy. Trollope comes, unconsciously, much nearer to the mark in Squire Dale, who keeps up an old place on a straitened income, or in Lord de Guest, in *The Small House at Allington*. *The Claverings* and *The Way We Live Now* are great novels, but little known.

Apart from his characterisation, Trollope had a few fixed ideas about young men and women, which run through all his novels. He thought it not only excusable, but normal that a young man should be in love with two and sometimes three young women at the same time. Phineas Finn, after he had buried his Irish wife, was in love with Lady Laura Kennedy, Lady Chiltern and Madame Max Goesler, if not quite simultaneously, very soon after one another. Harry Clavering is angrily in love with Julia Brabazon, who married Lord Ongar, and hardly had the church bells stopped, when he engages himself to plain Florence Burton. On the return from abroad of Lady Ongar, a rich and beautiful widow, now able to avow her love for Harry, the young fool wobbles for some time in Trollopian fashion, and finally sticks to Florence, whose brother, the architect, wipes his shoes with his handkerchief. Ralph Newton makes love to one cousin, proposes to another, is engaged to his tailor's daughter, and finally marries, or is married by, the daughter of a neighbouring squire. Trollope's common-sense realism taught him that the tearing, raging passion of which poets sing and novelists write is the creation of their fancy and has no existence in human nature. Love in young men he knew well enough was a transient, tepid, and if intense, then quickly changing emotion. But this fluency of feeling which he generously allowed to his young men, he forbade to his young women, who were all of the constant, clinging, quiet, much-enduring type, short, brown-haired and brown-eyed in appearance, like Florence Burton, Lucy Morris, Grace Crawley and Lucy Robarts. Constancy is, indeed, carried so far in Lily Dale as to amount to obstinacy, and many of his readers begged Trollope to allow the manly virtues of John Eames to be rewarded. But the slaughter of Mrs. Proudie was the utmost concession he would make to popular clamour. On girls who sold themselves for money or a title he had no mercy, and the punishment allotted to Lady Clavering, Julia Ongar and Laura Kennedy has always seemed to me to be too severe. Of all his young women, Mary Thorne is the most attractive.

Though Trollope called himself a Liberal, and under that label once contested the borough of Beverley, the following passage from *Doctor Thorne* discovers an attitude towards the landed aristocracy which to-day would be derided as antediluvian Toryism.

Writing of the Greshams of Greshamsbury, he says:

But the old symbols remained, and may such symbols long remain among us; they are still lovely and fit to be loved. They tell us of the true and manly feelings of other times; and to him who can read aright, they explain more fully, more truly than any written history can do, how Englishmen have become what they are. England is not yet a commercial country in the sense in which that epithet is used for her; and let us hope that she will not soon become so. She might surely as well be called feudal England or chivalrous England. If in Western civilised Europe there does still exist a nation among whom there are high signors, and with whom the owners of the land are the true aristocracy, the aristocracy that is trusted as being the best and fittest to rule, that nation is the English. Choose out the ten leading men of each great European people. Choose them in France, in Austria, Sardinia, Prussia, Russia, Sweden, Denmark, Spain, and then select the ten in England whose names are best known as those of leading statesmen; the result will show in which country there still exists the closest attachment to, the sincerest trust in, the old feudal and now so-called landed interests."

This passage reads romantically to-day, and yet it was written in my infancy by the most Victorian of novelists. Trollope's appreciation of the clerical aristocracy was no less hearty.

The dean was one of those old-world politicians— we meet them every day, and they are generally pleasant people—who enjoy the politics of the side to which they belong without any special belief in them. If pressed hard they will almost own that their so-called convictions are prejudices. But not for worlds would they be rid of them. When two or three of them meet together, they are as freemasons, who are bound by a pleasant bond which separates them from the outer world. They feel among themselves that every-thing that is being done is bad—even though that everything is done by their own party. . . . Education Bills and Irish Land Bills were all bad. Every step taken has been bad. And yet to them old England is of all countries in the world the best to live in, and is not at all the less comfortable because of the changes that have been made. These people are ready to grumble at every boon conferred on them, and yet to enjoy every boon. They know, too, their privileges, and, after a fashion, understand their position. It is picturesque, and it pleases them. To have been always in the right and yet always on the losing side; always being ruined, always under persecution from a wild spirit of republican demagogism—and yet never to lose anything, not even position or public esteem, is pleasant enough. A huge, living, daily increasing grievance that does one no palpable harm is the happiest possession a man can have. There is a large body of such men in England, and personally they are the salt of the nation. He who said that all Conservatives were stupid did not know them. Stupid Conservatives there may be—and there certainly are very stupid Radicals. The well-educated, widely-read Conservative, who is well assured that all good things are gradually being brought to an end by the voice of the people, is generally the pleasantest man to be met.

There is truth as well as humour in this portrait of the upper-class Conservative, drawn as it was more than half a century ago. Yet how far off it seems, like a page from the eighteenth century! This too was part of the Victorian Tradition.

XV

FRANK HARRIS

XV

FRANK HARRIS

WHEN I met Harris in the 'nineties he was deep
in magazine and newspaper dealings. He had just
sold the *Fortnightly Review*, which he had bought
and edited, in succession to Morley, and did it
very well. He had also edited, if not bought (but
of that I am not sure), the *Evening News*, which he
made a mess of, being too unpunctual, and he had
written *Montes the Matador* with great success. From
a barrister, whose name escapes me, the *Saturday
Review* was bought for a song—two or three
thousand pounds—and Frank was full of his new
toy, which he was editing in a way that made
the publishers wince. I met him one afternoon at
Lady Jeune's (as she was then), and so delighted
him by repeating George Eliot's saying that "You
must either give people what they're used to or
what they don't understand", that he carried me
off to a restaurant and bound me to his chariot,
there and then. The money for these deals he got
out of his wife's fortune. He had met the widow
of a North Country man of wealth in a Highland

castle, where he dominated by his tongue his hostess and her friend, who was unaccountably allowed to marry him without any settlement.

Either from insolence or genuine inability to mark time, he was seldom less than two hours late for an appointment. I asked him to lunch at the Café Royal at 1.30. As he was at that time worth six or seven hundred a year to me, I waited till 3, when he appeared without any apology. I invited him to dinner at Boodle's Club at 8.30, which I explained I had fixed late to suit him, and that he must be "on time". He came at 9.30, and lapped up the club's superb claret with smacking gusto, which he seemed to think would do for an apology. Harris quite recognised that his habits made him an impossible editor. However, before he quitted he did or tried to do his country one service. He wrote an editorial pointing out that between England and Germany war was inevitable, and was already beating up the sky.

Harris had an uncanny instinct, which would have made his fortune on the Stock Exchange, for choosing the precise hour "to stand from under", as the Americans say. He knew, none better, that the time to clear out had come. He chose the years between the Jameson Raid and the outbreak of the Boer War. He formed a company, and the first of his big shareholders was Alfred Beit. His arrangement of the share capital was new in this country, though it was common in the United States. He issued for cash 30,000 Preference shares and 2000 Deferred shares, which he allotted to himself, with a voting power of absolute control. Beit gave his cheque without troubling about figures or a balance sheet; he was anxious for a good Press. But for the group, consisting of Lord Hardwicke (the penultimate), the late Duke of Fife, and Lords Derby and Farquhar, some figures and a balance sheet were necessary, and they were of a remarkable kind. Even more important than circulation, so often fictitious, the advertisements are the assets which the purchaser of a paper most carefully scans. The three chief advertisers in the *Saturday* at the time were stated to be the Café Royal, a carriage-builder in Bond Street, and a firm of gun-makers in South Audley Street; but we could not trace any payments by any of them. On sending to inquire and ask for payment, if only on account, the directors were told: (1) By the Café Royal, that Mr. Harris had a large unpaid bill for luncheons and dinners, and that they had agreed to pay themselves by advertisements. When the bill had been worked off, the Café Royal would be happy, etc. (2) The coach-maker in Bond Street explained that Mr. Harris had bought a brougham and victoria for which he had not paid, and that the advertisements were being set off against the bill. (3) The gun-maker had just sold Mr. Harris a pair of guns, the price of which he was working off in advertisements, so that money was not to be thought of. The directors, of whom I was one, knew that they might have brought an action against Harris, but he had disappeared to the South of France, where we heard that he had invested his spoils in *The Hermitage*, then being started in Monte Carlo.

There followed the Boer War, and five years later Hardwicke died, the group lost their money, and the *Review* was sold to Sir Gervase Beckett. Only once again did I run up against Frank Harris, at Brighton, in 1910, or 1911, when he scowled, and said something disagreeable about my looking old, and the *Review* going to pot.

The only human beings of the male sex that Harris seemed to be fond of were Harold Frederic, the American novelist, a Christian scientist, and Oscar Wilde, to whom he showed genuine kindness. The doubts that I have heard thrown upon

Harris's authorship of *The Elder Conkling*, which some said was written by Frederic, appear absurd to anyone who had heard Harris talk. He talked indeed better than he wrote, and to my taste better than Oscar Wilde, because he was really spontaneous, whereas Wilde's epigrams always wore an air of preparation, though of course some of his best ones could not have been so; for instance, his reply to the man who asked him what he should do about the conspiracy of silence against his books, "Join it, you fool, join it". Harris was no niggard with his wit. He would pour out his words just as generously when he was alone with you as when he had an audience. This was one of his good points. I remember his declaiming for a couple of hours to convince me that words were more important than deeds. One of his victims said ruefully to me, "His talk stimulates me like champagne"; and luckily its effect was as evanescent.

What Frank Harris did in America during the war, until 1917, and his subsequent obscured sulphurous existence in France, the world knows as well as I. A foolish and gushing American wrote to ask me to contribute to a Life of Frank Harris which he was preparing. I replied by asking him whether he had read the Autobiography. The rest is silence, except that I remember reading on the flyleaf of the copy that was lent me the name of one of the best known of American editors and publicists.

XVI

QUEEN VICTORIA'S MIDDLE YEARS

XVI

QUEEN VICTORIA'S MIDDLE YEARS

THE interest of Mr. Buckle's edition of Queen Victoria's letters [1] is somewhat marred by the obvious fact that they are the remainder-biscuit out of a chest that has been ransacked by rapacious experts. Mr. Buckle himself in his six volumes of the Life of Disraeli is admittedly the chief of these raiders; Lord Morley, in his three volumes on Gladstone, is a good second; while following in their wake we have the Life of Lord Granville by Lord Fitz-Maurice, the Life of Lord Clarendon by Sir Herbert Maxwell, the lives of Archbishop Tait and Lord Cranbrook, and last, but by no means least, Sir Sidney Lee's *King Edward VII*.

These are heavy drafts upon the Windsor Archives; so that presumably Mr. Buckle's volumes are meant to evolve for the instruction of the public a still more intimate view of Queen Victoria's character. If that be the intention, I cannot help saying that many of the letters written in the first years of the Queen's widowhood had

[1] *Letters of Queen Victoria, 1862-1878.*

better not have been published. Why dwell upon
the weakest and most unhappy period of anybody's
life in detail? The great Queen is seen at her
worst in the six years that followed the death of
the Prince Consort. I feel about some of her
letters of this volume very much what I felt about
the publication of the senile love-letters of Lord
Beaconsfield. In both cases one or two letters
would surely have been enough. That the Queen
of England, at the age of forty-two, in the very
prime of life, surrounded by a large and affectionate family, guided in political business by the
most courageous and sagacious statesmen in the
world, ruling over a loyal and prosperous Empire,
should describe herself as a crushed, lone, helpless
widow whose one wish was to follow her husband
to a better world, is undignified, and unworthy of
her station. The exaggerated language in which
Victoria paints her morbid passion of bereavement
is not only addressed to her relatives and her
children, but to her Ministers, to Palmerston,
Russell and Gladstone. In her later years the
Queen showed great power of self-restraint, of
endurance, and determination. There was only one
living person, perhaps, who could have taught the
Queen the duty of controlling these feelings,

namely, her uncle, King Leopold, who unfortunately encouraged her in what was really a form
of self-indulgence. These early letters are written
in a stilted and hysterical style; and after pages of
them, it was with unspeakable delight that I came
across a letter from "Vicky" (the Crown Princess
of Prussia) who writes: "Things here are in such a
mess as never was". There was another prejudice
which contributed greatly to the Queen's un-
popularity in these years. A Sovereign who is
afraid of crowds is like a sailor who is sea-sick, or
a nurse who faints at the sight of blood. Victoria
was afraid of crowds in her early widowhood, and
consequently hated London, and would never, if
she could possibly help it, sleep so much as a night
at Buckingham Palace, always returning after her
Drawing-rooms in the afternoon to Windsor.
Londoners bitterly resented this avoidance of their
city, of which they are justly proud. Even Windsor
Castle, the glory of England, the Queen wrote of
as "a living grave".

Nor can it be said that the historical interest of
the events with which the Queen was called upon
to cope is absorbing, for the simple reason that
the ground has been traversed over and over again
in the very biographies to which I have above

alluded. Indeed, whoever writes about the Duchies of Schleswig-Holstein should be heavily fined. We all know that Russell and Palmerston made fools of themselves about the Duchies, having first strutted before Europe as the protectors of Denmark, and having finally sneaked out of the consequences of their words. Devoted as she was to Alexandra, Princess of Wales, the Queen was decidedly pro-Prussian at the outset of the quarrel, though after the annexation, and still more after the war upon Austria in 1866, she began to write to Vicky about the "infamy of Prussia". The best letters in the volume are those of the Crown Princess, afterwards the Empress Frederick, who gives a vivid, but just, account of her difficult position under the eye of Bismarck. Queen Victoria's views on the foreign politics of Europe, written to her daughter, to the Kings of Prussia and Belgium, and to her Ministers, are sound and well expressed; but it is lamentable to observe how little effect they had on the course of events.

It will interest the present generation to know Queen Victoria's real opinion of Lord Palmerston. Just after his death she wrote to her uncle, the King of the Belgians:

He had many valuable qualities, though many bad ones, and we had, God knows, terrible trouble with him over foreign affairs. Still, as Prime Minister, he managed affairs at home well, and behaved to me well; but I never liked him, or could ever the least respect him, nor could I forget his conduct on a certain occasion to my Angel. He was very vindictive, and personal feeling influenced his political acts very much.

It was only when, in 1866, the Conservatives turned out Gladstone on the Reform Bill, that the Queen began to be aware of Disraeli. In an extract from her Journal, which, by the way, is more interesting than her letters, the Queen notes:

Saw Mr. Disraeli after tea, who spoke of the great Reform meeting on the 3rd, also of reform in general. . . . He was amiable, and clever, but is a strange man.

Strange indeed must that exotic figure have seemed in the prim circle of a Victorian Court! But it is extraordinary how Victoria expanded and mellowed under the warmth of Disraeli's sympathy and tact. Here was a second, though a very different, and more stimulating, Lord Melbourne! In a long letter to Her Majesty in 1868, arguing against the promotion of Tait from London to Canterbury, there is one of Disraeli's most characteristic touches: "There is in his idiosyncrasy a strange fund of enthusiasm, a quality which ought never to be possessed by an Archbishop of Canterbury or a Prime Minister of England. The Bishop of London sympathises with everything that is earnest; but what is earnest is not always true; on the contrary, error is often more earnest than truth." What could Victoria have thought of this cynicism? In no department of her duties did the Queen's common sense and knowledge of men come out more strongly than in the ecclesiastical appointments, where she nearly always opposed Disraeli, who had the sagacity to yield.

Queen Victoria has often been praised for brains and influence which she did not possess. It is said, for instance, that her letters show her to have been a great foreign stateswoman. The surprising thing is that, considering her position as a Sovereign of what was at that time the greatest empire in the world, and considering her relationships, she had in fact so little influence upon the great political events that occurred during her reign. Her grandfather was the King of Hanover, as was her uncle, and her daughter was married to the Crown Prince of Prussia, afterwards Emperor of Germany. Her husband was a member of the House of Coburg. If anywhere, Queen Victoria ought to have had a favourable hearing in Germany, and some influence over the policy of that country. As a matter of fact she had none. Victoria was an honest woman, and she said openly that Germany was the country of her family, for which she had a natural predilection. At the opening of the Schleswig-Holstein dispute she was pro-German, although not to the length of going to war; but when she saw the design of Bismarck to annex those countries, she began to protest. She wrote familiar letters to the King of Prussia, who was a noodle, and who handed her letters to Bismarck, and we can imagine the sneer with which the man of blood and iron read the Englishwoman's plaintive efforts on the side of peace. Ten years later, at the outbreak of the Franco-German War, Queen Victoria, with all her information from inside sources, like the letters of her daughter the Crown Princess, was as much in the dark as the man in the street as to the real origin of the conflict. On the surface it appeared that the French were the aggressors, and therefore the majority of the people with their Sovereign were pro-

German. It was not till long afterwards that the world discovered that Bismarck had secretly instigated the Hohenzollern candidature for the throne of Spain, and had mutilated or forged the Ems telegram which led to the declaration of war by France. After Sedan and during the siege of Paris, Victoria wrote nice kindly letters to the new Emperor and his wife Augusta, and to her daughter, urging clemency and generosity upon the conquerors, without the slightest effect upon the conduct of Moltke and Bismarck. It may be admitted that Queen Victoria helped by writing to the Tsar of Russia and to her own Ministers to prevent the monstrous crime of a second war on France in 1875, which there is no doubt that Bismarck contemplated. But the British and Russian Governments had decided to stop it, and the man who contributed to the result more than anyone else was Sir Robert Morier, who on his way to St. Petersburg as Ambassador had a royal procession through France as *l'homme qui roulait Bismarck*.

In the Turko-Russian War of 1877 Queen Victoria took a very violent part against Russia. There can be no doubt that if the Queen had had her way, and had wielded the power which her panegyrists ascribe to her, she would have plunged

England into war on the side of the Turk. Lord Beaconsfield has told us that while the negotiations which ended in the Berlin Congress were going on, the Queen wrote to him every day, and telegraphed to him every hour, and this he said to Lady Bradford was a literal fact. But greatly as one must admire the courage, the clear decision, and the determination of the Queen to make England's power felt abroad, I cannot see that her vehement outpourings had any real effect upon the course of politics. Against the rock of Lord Derby's sullen impassivity the waves of royal wrath broke in vain. The Foreign Secretary stiffened his back, thrust out his under lip, and did nothing. Lord Beaconsfield, it is hardly necessary to say, was far too clever to go to war when he could get what he wanted by threatening to go to war. At all periods of his life Disraeli was under the sway of feminine influence. When he was at the meridian of his career, driving Russia back from the gates of Constantinople, calling out the reserves, summoning black troops from India, and secretly acquiring Cyprus as a military station, he was in love with three women simultaneously, and all of them, as Schouvaloff observed, grandmothers. It may well be that our Prime Minister persuaded himself that his Royal Mistress guided and inspired his foreign policy; but the world still smiles at the delusion.

In domestic politics the strong character and decided views of Queen Victoria naturally had a greater influence, though not so much as we are asked to believe. It may surprise those who, like the late Lord Salisbury, were wont to abuse Disraeli for his "leap in the dark" in 1867, that the Franchise Bill was really forced upon the Conservative Party by the Queen, who was determined that this matter, having been played with by many Governments for so many years, should be settled. The Queen certainly interfered frequently and forcibly in the distribution of ecclesiastical patronage. She was decidedly Broad Church and would have liked to appoint nobody but Stanleys and Bradleys, which would have created an uproar. She despised the Low Church as "evangelical trash", and she roundly denounced the High Church party as Romanists in disguise. However, she prevented Disraeli from using Church appointments as a means to political influence.

Most of her critics miss the real greatness of Queen Victoria, which was neither political nor ecclesiastical, but social.

Insensibly, by no show of provincial puritanism, but by innate elevation of character, Victoria lifted the moral tone of England, and by mere simplicity contrived to surround reserve and dullness with the prestige of the eighteenth century. That she did it by herself is proved by the fact that her first mentors were an old *roué* and a German youth, who cannot have contributed to the result. The Queen made reception at her Court what she meant it to be, the recognition of rank, ability and virtue.

On the subject of honours Queen Victoria entertained the strongest views, of which there are instances in her correspondence. She was pressed to confer a peerage on Chief Justice Cockburn, and refused because of his "notoriously bad moral character". Lord Granville answered jauntily, not to the Queen but to Sir Charles Phipps, that "Sir A. Cockburn was immoral as a young man in one line. He has two illegitimate children, and anyway he was no worse than Brougham or Lyndhurst."

Cockburn was told of the Queen's objection, and being unmarried gave up the idea of a peerage. Some years later, after the Alabama Arbitration, he was given the Grand Cross of the Bath.

An instance of Whiggish exclusiveness occurred when Disraeli went out of office in 1868, and when Victoria, who was really anxious to gratify him, asked what he wanted for himself. Disraeli asked that his wife should be made Viscountess Beaconsfield in her own right. The Queen was much embarrassed, and the Court thrown into giggles. We learn from General Grey that the hesitation was caused by a friendly fear lest the couple should become the object of endless ridicule. There you have the Whig point of view. Mrs. Disraeli a Viscountess, how absurd! Needless to say that when it was done, nobody saw anything ridiculous in it, and Lady Beaconsfield wrote the Queen a very pretty and dignified letter. It should also be remembered that General Grey had been Dizzy's successful opponent at Wycombe thirty-five years ago, and his memory was probably haunted by the vision of the Jew boy in pink waistcoat and velvet pantaloons, denouncing from the portico of the Red Lion Whigs in general and Greys and Caringtons in particular.

It was as a great lady who banished from the Court the horrors and scandals of her two predecessors, that Victoria deserves to be placed on a pedestal in history. Middle-class careerists and those who broke the marriage vow, were not received at Court, and would never have dreamed of attempting to get there. License, vulgarity and pretentiousness stood abashed in Queen Victoria's reign, and the subordination which is vital to the existence of society was preserved.

XVII

DISRAELI'S MERIDIAN

XVII

DISRAELI'S MERIDIAN

EVEN middle-age cannot make Disraeli uninteresting, as all who have read Mr. Buckle's biography of him will agree. In a well-known passage of *Sibyl* Disraeli muses on the fact that there are certain historical personages over whom "a mysterious oblivion is encouraged to creep", and his instance of a "suppressed character" is Lord Shelburne. There seems no danger of oblivion creeping over Disraeli any more than over Samuel Johnson, or Buonaparte, or Chatham. Why are some individuals perennially interesting, while others, more powerful, perhaps, or more successful in their lives, fall into "the dusty crypt of darkened forms and faces"? What are the qualities that arrest the attention of a man's contemporaries and of posterity? Many poets, painters, philosophers, scientists are only discovered after their death. It is different with statesmen and soldiers. But many party leaders, like the second Pitt, Peel, Gladstone, absorb public attention while they live, and after their death become mere names, pegs on which the historian hangs a tale. The striking thing about Disraeli is that, largely as he loomed in the eye of his contemporaries, the interest in his career and character grows stronger with the lapse of time. Has any other statesman been put upon the stage within thirty-five years of his death? Yet in the middle of a fearful war people went to see the play and read the book which Mr. Buckle has composed with so much dramatic skill and historical insight. What is the secret of Disraeli's posthumous popularity?

There are many reasons. Disraeli was the first pure-bred Hebrew who attained to supreme political power. There have been financial Jews ever since the world began—thousands of them— and there have been musical, artistic, literary Jews by the hundred. But never before did a Jew "break his birth's invidious bar" with such force as to rule a world-wide Empire. This is a point of great historical interest. In a letter to Mary Gladstone at the moment of Lord Beaconsfield's death Lord Acton wrote: "The *Pall Mall resumés* of Lord Beaconsfield have been intensely interesting. None seemed to me too severe, but some were shocking at the moment. He was quite remarkable enough to fill a column of Eloge. Some one wrote to me yesterday that no Jew for 1800 years has played so great a part in the world. That would be no Jew since St. Paul; and it is very startling. But, putting aside literature, and, therefore, Spinoza and Heine, almost simultaneously with Disraeli, a converted Jew, Stahl, a man without birth or fortune, became the leader of the Prussian Conservative and aristocratic Party.

"He led them from about 1850 to 1860, when he died; and he was intellectually far superior to Disraeli—I should say the greatest reasoner that has ever served the Conservative cause. But he never obtained power or determined any important event. Lassalle died after two years of agitation. Benjamin, the soul of the Confederate Ministry, now rising to the first rank of English lawyers, had too short and too disastrous a public career. In short, I have not yet found an answer." This is characteristic, for who but Lord Acton ever heard of Stahl? Another source of attraction was the unlikeness of Disraeli to everybody else—in appearance, manners, speech and thought. The nickname of "Old Oddity" gained a good deal of Dr. Johnson's celebrity. I was present at the debate in the House of Lords when Lord Beaconsfield explained the Treaty of Berlin.

> With grave
> Aspect he rose, and in his rising seem'd
> A pillar of State: deep on his front engraven
> Deliberation sat, and public care.

He divided his speech into two parts, the first dealing with Europe, the second treating of the Eastern possessions of the Sultan. After dismissing the absurd pretensions of Greece with a counsel of patience, he stopped and put his hand into the inner breast-pocket of his frock-coat. He pulled out a tiny silver flask, deliberately unscrewed the top, took a pull at its contents, as deliberately replaced it, and turning to a grave and silent House said, "And now, my lords, I will ask you to accompany me into Asia". A well-bred ripple ran along the scarlet benches.

It was impossible not to be struck with his superiority to the surrounding peers. As he spoke, somehow or other the Granvilles, the Derbys, and the Salisburys seemed to shrink into conventional mediocrities. Bagehot will have it that Disraeli's mind was intensely receptive of immediate impressions, but unoriginal, uncreative. Bagehot was fond of paradoxes, and this is one of his most foolish. The education of our public schools and universities has indisputable merits, but it has the fault of turning out its pupils in a conventional mould. Disraeli had not learned to speak at "Pop" or the Union; he taught himself on the hustings and rehearsed in his father's library. It was his detachment from the vulgar prejudices of the upper and middle classes, his isolated and purely literary upbringing, that gave freshness and force to his speculations on politics.

A large number of persons in all parties—Whigs, Tories, Radicals and "Gigadibs the literary man"; Carlyle, Bagehot, Gladstone, Bright, Robert Cecil, Acton, Beresford Hope; the *Saturday*, *Edinburgh* and *Quarterly Reviews* all combined to spread the legend that Disraeli was a wicked and immoral man. They shook their heads over his shiftiness, and gossiped about his debts. They could not have contributed more surely and effectively to the popular interest in his career. For who does not care more about Becky Sharp than about Amelia or Laura? Thackeray intended that we should love Amelia and despise Becky. But Amelia and Laura are bores with their virtue and meekness, while we follow with the keenest interest, not always distinguishable from admiration, the turns and shifts and plots and combinations with which the dauntless Becky fought the

world from the bandbox in Curzon Street. Nothing excites curiosity and sympathy so strongly
as the suspicion of skeletons in the cupboard,
of secret debts, of struggles behind the curtain.
Gladstone was a pattern of propriety and prosperity. He never swore; he shuddered at the smell
of tobacco; he frowned at a Rabelaisian anecdote;
he probably never had a debt in his life. That is
why his biography, apart from his public transactions, is quite uninteresting, and will be read by
nobody a hundred years hence. As for his
superiority over his rival in the matter of unselfishness and public virtue, Mr. Buckle has
effectively dispelled that legend.

It appears that not once, but twice or thrice,
Disraeli offered to give up to Gladstone the lead
of the House of Commons if he would join the
Conservative Party, which at that time he supported by his voice and pen. The celebrated letter
is too long to quote, but I believe everyone will
admit that it is a model of manly self-effacement
and chivalrous obeisance to a rival. It made no
impression on Gladstone; he had other and longer
views; he was far too astute to be touched by his
rival's generous impulse; he coldly declined Disraeli's offer. If there was one man whom Glad-

stone abused in private and resolutely opposed in public it was Lord Palmerston. In 1859 Gladstone supported Lord Derby's Government against the vote of want of confidence, and a few weeks later accepted the post of Chancellor of the Exchequer in Palmerston's Government. The reason was plain. Palmerston was verging on his eightieth year; Russell was nearly as old; Gladstone saw that if he joined the Liberals he *must* succeed to the leadership, and so he joined them. And yet Gladstone was regarded by his contemporaries as a pattern of public virtue, while Disraeli was treated to "thimble-rigger", "conjurer", "charlatan", "self-seeking adventurer".

We see things more clearly now, and Disraeli gains much by the contrast with the unctuous rectitude of his great opponent. The crowning quality of Disraeli's attractiveness was his wit. "With words", said Mephistopheles to Faust, "you can do everything"; and certainly Disraeli's power over the English language is only comparable to Byron's. England, like all democracies, is governed by words; but witty words have always been rare, and seem nowadays to have disappeared. Gladstone governed by words, as did Asquith, but in neither was there a spark of wit or humour;

and even the Irish have grown dull. For sheer wit
and irresistible drollery Disraeli's speech at Slough
on the collapse of Cardwell's vote of censure cannot be beaten, and has never even been approached
in political literature. Who could be long or
seriously angry with a man who rejoiced, in the
heat of the Reform battle, that a "good broad
piece of furniture separated him from Gladstone";
who described Lord Shaftesbury as "Gamaliel
himself with the broad phylacteries of faction on
his forehead"; who spoke of "the stately cynicism"
of Sir James Graham and "the Batavian grace" of
Mr. Beresford Hope; who pictured the Treasury
Bench as a "row of extinct volcanoes"; and who
dismissed Peel's hackneyed quotations with the
remark that "they were the better appreciated because most of them had already received the meed
of Parliamentary approbation".

The pregnant lesson which Disraeli's meridian
should convey to the present generation is the
value, or, rather, the necessity, of a powerful
leader of the Opposition. Three-fourths of Disraeli's life were spent in the position in which, as
Mr. Buckle teaches us by inexpugnable records, he
shared the cares, though not the cash or the credit,
of Government. This unfair partition of rewards

and punishments was not of Disraeli's choosing, though he saw clearly the reason of it. Palmerston was a Conservative in the skin of a Liberal. The middle class, then the rulers of England, knew this, and were content that Palmerston should check the Radicals, and that Disraeli should check Palmerston and Russell in their foreign policy. Lord Derby also knew it, and with his racing and his Lancashire rents in his pocket, was content to visit the House of Lords between his fits of gout and fire an occasional broadside into "old Pam". But Disraeli was naturally far from contented, as is shown by the following passage from a draft letter to Horsman, written in 1859, just before the fall of the second Derby Administration: "If the usual combination throws us out, Lord Palmerston is to be the next man, and will form a Government with his friends, and is to be supported, not generally, but invariably, by mine sitting opposite to him. I have no doubt he will govern the country well, but I do not see why he should do it better than us, nor do I see why this hocus-pocus should be perpetually repeated." It was to avoid the impending fate of this perpetual hocus-pocus that Disraeli made such frantic attempts to get Graham, Gladstone or Palmerston to join forces with him. *Dis aliter visum*: it was not to be. Of Disraeli's controlling influence over the foreign policy of the country from the Opposition Bench there are proofs on every page of history. Disraeli was the first statesman to establish the patriotic doctrine that it is the duty of an Opposition to support the Government in the prosecution of a war, provided the Government does prosecute it earnestly. He took no party advantage of Roebuck's Committee to inquire into the scandalous mismanagement of the Crimean War. But as soon as he saw that there was nothing more to be gained by the war, he pressed the Government, in the teeth of a bellicose Press and angry public, to make an early peace, as they did. The Indian Mutiny broke out under Palmerston's Government, which followed the Aberdeen Coalition. With a prescience as rare as the courage by which it was supported, Disraeli set himself against the policy of vindictiveness which the massacre of Cawnpore and the siege of Lucknow and Delhi excited in this country. Luckily, on the sudden expulsion of Palmerston from office, the settlement of India fell into the hands of the Derby Government. Disraeli, in a minority of the House of

Commons, after literally laughing Palmerston and his satellites out of court, modified Lord Canning's policy of confiscation in Oude, and transferred the Government of India from "John Company" to the Secretary of State in Council. When we read Bagehot's sneer at Disraeli's constructive capacity, and remember his epigram that "Disraeli's chaff was exquisite, but his wheat was poor stuff", let us correct it by remembering that in a brief year's tenure of office without a majority Disraeli created the system by which our Indian Empire is governed at this hour. Before passing from this topic of Disraeli's creative or legislative power, let me add that in 1867, when Disraeli was in office for two years and a half, again without a majority, he placed upon the Statute Book the British North American Act, which provided the Dominion of Canada with the charter of its liberty and progress. It is literal truth to say that in three years, while wrestling with a factious majority, Disraeli did more for the British Empire than Palmerston and Gladstone achieved in fifty years, supported as they were by a complaisant Press and their well-disciplined battalions in the House of Commons. Over the reckless and often ridiculous European policy of Russell and

Palmerston a very salutary control was exercised by Disraeli.

Disraeli's career reached its zenith with his great personal triumph in 1867, and his accession to the Premiership on the retirement of Lord Derby in 1868. With regard to the once vexed question of Parliamentary reform, Disraeli was neither better nor worse than his opponents. It is impossible to read the insincere manœuvres of the two parties on the extension of the franchise without thinking of what Halifax said of the quarrels of Whigs and Tories in the seventeenth century about religion —"it is like two men quarrelling about a woman for whom neither cares a pin". As Bulwer Lytton said of the Reform Bill of 1859: "Nine out of ten said loudly 'We must have a Reform Bill'; but eight out of every nine whispered to each other, 'Does anyone want one?' "

Palmerston certainly did not, and though he allowed Russell to bring in three Bills, he allowed each of them to be rejected. Disraeli, of course, saw that if he suffered the Liberal Party to establish a monopoly of Parliamentary Reform, he might as well retire from politics and leave his party to disappear as completely as the Tories disappeared for fifty-five years after Bolingbroke's

flight in 1715. He accordingly brought in two
Bills, which the Liberals threw out. Such was the
state of the Reform question when Palmerston's
death in 1865 removed the real obstruction. Then
the game began in earnest. Gladstone, the ex-
Tory, brought in his Bill for lowering the borough
franchise to £7 rental. Disraeli defeated his Bill
by splitting up the Liberal majority of seventy,
and took Gladstone's place as Chancellor of the
Exchequer. The prime movers of the Reform Bill
of 1867 were the Queen and Lord Derby, while
Disraeli, having just won a great battle, was disposed to rest his weary limbs in "the warm pre-
cincts of the Treasury". But the Queen was in-
sistent to have this great question settled; she
pressed Lord Derby, who pressed the war-worn
Disraeli. Such was the genesis of "the leap in the
dark", the great Tory-Radical Reform Act which
swept away all rental qualifications and introduced
bare household franchise. It has been argued that
the result of the Reform Act of 1867 was to place
the Conservatives in power for twenty-four out of
forty-eight years. It is a shallow observation. It
was not household suffrage but Parnell who gave
Lord Salisbury and Mr. Balfour eighteen years
of office. The Queen purred and Lord Derby

chuckled over "the dishing of the Whigs". What did Disraeli himself think? Disraeli was remarkably tenacious of his ideas. In *The Spirit of Whiggism*, written in 1836, Disraeli had argued that we never would have democracy in this country, no matter how extended the suffrage, so long as the distribution of property was unaltered, and the distribution of property would never be altered by a people who worshipped wealth and reverenced law. We know better to-day; but Disraeli could not foresee the Finance Act of 1909, or the Great War. In 1867 he doubtless thought that household suffrage was a safe experiment. However we may differ about democracy, we must all "pursue the triumph and partake the gale" of this extraordinary life. We leave Disraeli in the meridian of his career, toasted amidst the frantic cheers of the Carlton Club, welcomed—which he valued more —by the ecstasy of his devoted wife, and promoted by a smiling Sovereign to the highest honour a subject can enjoy.

Ten years later Lord Beaconsfield, "the centre of the world's desire", was Prime Minister, not alone of England, but of Europe. When he returned from Berlin and drove through cheering crowds to Downing Street, his mind must have jumped the half-century and dwelt on his first novel, *Vivian Grey*, and his first speech in Parliament, "I have begun many things, and have often failed, but I have always succeeded at last".

XVIII

BURKE: THE FOUNDER OF CONSERVATISM

XVIII

BURKE: THE FOUNDER OF CONSERVATISM

ACCORDING to the best authority Edmund Burke was born at Dublin in 1729, his father being a Protestant solicitor and his mother a Roman Catholic. As Matthew Arnold has too justly reproached us with ignorance of our English classics, let us remind ourselves of some points in the career of the greatest political thinker and speaker of the eighteenth century. Indeed, so much did Burke say and do of note in thirty-two years of public life (1765 to 1797) that no modern has dared to write his biography. All the great writers and historians have shied at a Life of Burke as beyond the compass of a Macaulay and a Carlyle. We content ourselves with Payne's very able Introduction to the Clarendon Press edition of the *Select Works*; with Morley's monograph; with Hazlitt's two essays, one attacking Burke as a mad incendiary, the tool of despotism, and the other bowing to him as the greatest philosopher and literary artist that ever lived; and with essays and allusions from Arnold, Disraeli and Mr. Birrell. Sir James Prior's Life (1826) is too much neglected, for though enthusiastic and a little rambling in chronology, as was the old-fashioned way, it is full, and written in a well-bred style, and contains many interesting anecdotes, some of which I have used in these pages.

Burke arrived in London in 1750, his twenty-first year, with empty pockets and a crowded brain, and, what did not add to his prospects, an Irish brogue. He never alluded in after life to the squalid struggle of his first ten years, not because he was a snob, but because he had a stately mind, and was determined like Disraeli to "play the great game", even with borrowed money. There was a kindred recklessness between Burke's purchase of Gregories, a manor-house with six hundred acres near Beaconsfield, and Disraeli's purchase of Hughenden. In both transactions the purchase was made by mortgage supplemented by a loan, in Burke's case from the Marquess of Rockingham, in Disraeli's from the Bentinck family. And in both cases the wonder was, not how the purchase money was found, but where the income to keep the thing going was procured. When Dr. Johnson was shown over the new house, he quoted "*Haud equidem invideo; miror magis*", which I have always thought had a double meaning—"Beautiful! but how the deuce do you do it, 'Mund Burke?"

Another point of coincidence between this illustrious pair is worth recalling. Three years before his death Burke was offered a peerage, and in Stanhope's *Life of Pitt* (p. 244, vol. ii) we are told that "already was the title chosen as Lord Beaconsfield. Already was the patent preparing." The coronet never came, because Burke's son died at that moment, and the father was obviously in declining health. With the melodramatic pathos which is the prerogative of genius, the situation is thus described:

The storm has gone over me, and I lie like one of those old oaks which the late hurricane has scattered about me. I am stripped of all my honours; I am torn up by the roots and lie prostrate on the earth. I am alone. I have none to meet my enemies in the gate. I live in an inverted order. They who ought to have succeeded me have gone before me. They who ought to have been to me as posterity are in the place of ancestors.

It is well known that Burke thought his son a cleverer man than himself.

Though Burke enjoyed fully the social inter-course which his position in the inner circle of Whig politics brought him, his private life is on the whole a painful and rather humiliating spec-tacle. That under the instigation of his cousin and his brother he gambled heavily in East India stock is improbable, because Will and Richard were certainly ruined, while Edmund maintained the equilibrium of his impecuniosity. But it has to be admitted that in money matters Burke, like so many men of genius, especially Irishmen, Sheridan for instance, had little sense of delicacy. He borrowed from Garrick, and from Reynolds, and when Dr. Brocklesby made him a present of £1000, he acknowledged it with a majestic blend of independence and gratitude. Among Lord Rockingham's papers was found Burke's bond for £30,000, with a direction that it should be can-celled. Lord Fitzwilliam, the executor, in return-ing the bond to Burke, wrote that the transaction was equally honourable to his dead and to his living friend.

I am afraid that England no longer breeds great gentlemen like Rockingham and Fitzwilliam. At the same time, it should be remembered that the Whigs owed Burke a great debt, no less than the restoration of the moral tone of their party. He educated the inarticulate aristocrats of the eighteenth century as Disraeli educated the Tory squires of the nineteenth century. For when we turn from the private to the public life of Burke, the record is one of stupendous achievement, marred by faults of temper, but unspotted by any act of meanness or treachery. Someone introduced Burke in 1765 to Lord Rockingham, the honest, clear-headed, but speechless leader of one of those Whig gangs which, after the fall of Walpole, squabbled and intrigued over the Government of England for forty-three years. The Rockingham gang having beaten the Bloomsbury gang, were in office for a year, and popped Burke in for the borough of Wendover. In March 1766 we have Johnson writing to Bennet Langton: "However I will tell you that the Club subsists; but we have the loss of Burke's company since he has been engaged in public business, in which he has gained more reputation than perhaps any man at his first appearance ever gained before. He made two speeches in the House for repealing the Stamp Act, which were publicly commended by Mr. Pitt, and have filled the town with wonder. Burke is a great man by nature, and is expected soon to attain civil greatness." He spoke a few days after taking his seat, and from that date to his death in 1797 Burke's name was the head and front of the three great questions of the latter half of the eighteenth century: the war with the American colonies, the impeachment of Warren Hastings and the French Revolution. Added to these as side-shows, though each of them was sufficient to occupy the whole time of an ordinary politician, were the grievances of the Irish Catholics under the jobbery of the Ponsonbys and Beresfords, and the cause of economy in the public service.

If Bacon took all knowledge to be his province, Burke took all government to be his. "There are only two things Burke doesn't understand," said W. G. Hamilton, "gaming and music", and they are outside politics. To say that he was always in the right in his great causes would be too much. Lord Morley said to a friend shortly before his death that the history of Burke's advocacy of the American colonies against the King and Parliament ought to be written. It ought to be, though Morley's saying is dark. Burke was the paid agent of the American colonies, receiving six or seven hundred a year to place their case before the English nation. It was, to say the least, an ambiguous position, though the reasoning and eloquence of the two speeches on the American question are incomparable. George III was right about the American rebels. With competent admirals and generals, and a Secretary of State less disgracefully careless than Lord George Germain, the United States might now be a part of the British Empire. In the case of Warren Hastings, Burke's merit was, not that he proved his charges, or that he conducted the prosecution with the dignity and fairness befitting the occasion, for he did neither, but that he forced the English nation to think about their government of Eastern peoples, that he created a colonial conscience. In his opposition to the French Revolution—"a voice like the Apocalypse sounded over England, and even echoed in all the courts of Europe"— I think that Burke was in the right. But then I am a Tory. Burke was amply avenged on the Whigs for keeping him out of their Cabinets, for in his secession to Pitt he took with him Portland, Fitzwilliam and Windham.

Much has been said for and against Burke's style. Its frequent extravagances offended Matthew Arnold, who thought Addison the model, and sniffed at some of Burke's ebullitions as Asiatic.

The violence of his attacks upon Jacobinism so annoyed young John Morley that he could find in the *Letters on a Regicide Peace* nothing but "gulfs of empty words, reckless phrases and senseless vituperations". It must be remembered that Burke was a pure-bred Irishman, and the Irish have never understood the literary effect of understatement. In the House of Commons Burke was frequently provoked into errors of taste and judgement. Wilkes said that as the Venus of Apelles suggested milk and honey, so Burke's oratory occasionally suggested whisky and potatoes, and Wilkes, though he played to the gallery as a demagogue, was a cultivated man. The scene in the House of Commons when Burke flung a sample knife made in Birmingham for the Jacobins on the floor, with an exhortation to his audience to "keep French principles from their heads and French daggers from their hearts", was a trifle too dramatic, but it was only Sheridan's gibe about "the fork being forgotten" that has preserved it as an absurdity. The truth is that Burke was unsuited to a popular assembly. His voice was harsh, his brogue was strong, and he was terribly long. His large spectacles, then unusual, his tight and ill-fitting brown coat, and the little bob-wig with curls, excited the derision of the dandies from White's and Brookes's. The general election of 1784, which was Pitt's triumph, brought in a crowd of young Tories, to whom Burke was anything but an object of reverence. It was his worst period; he was in the trough of the sea. The Fox–North coalition had just been broken up; the impeachment of Warren Hastings was beginning; both were unpopular, and the French Revolution, which was to make him the idol of the Tories, was still in the unopened book of fate. It is sad but not surprising to read that Burke's speeches were often drowned by coughing, cracking of nuts and sucking of oranges.

In the ordinary sense of the term Burke was not an orator. An eminent critic, in comparing the two statesmen, wrote: "Chatham supplied his hearers with motives to immediate action. Burke furnished them with reasons for action, which might have little effect upon them at the time, but for which they would be the wiser and better all their lives after." His speeches are writings, and so far from being flowery or verbose, Burke is one of the severest writers. If he multiplies words, it is not from want of ideas, but because he is trying to put his ideas before you as variously and as forcibly as he can. It may be true that often "he treads the brink of all we hate", but he never goes over the edge. Hazlitt has written the best things on Burke's style, bitterly as he hated his Tory politics: "He is the most poetical of our prose writers, and at the same time his prose never degenerates into the mere effeminacy of poetry; for he always aims at over-powering rather than pleasing; and consequently sacrifices beauty and delicacy to force and vividness. He has invariably a task to perform, a positive purpose to execute, an effect to produce. His only object is therefore to strike hard and in the right place; if he misses his mark, he repeats his blow; and does not care how ungraceful the action, or how clumsy the instrument, provided it brings down his antagonist." This is the answer to the finical criticism of Arnold, and the prim horror of Morley.

It has been objected to Burke's Toryism that it was largely emotional. Burke's imagination was warm, but it was not confused. He never denied, still less derided, the sufferings of the French people: but he knew that the murder of the king and queen, and the plundering of the Church and the aristocracy, would not relieve a starving peasantry; just as we see to-day that the wholesale

massacre and robbery of princes, priests, land-
owners and middle-class by the Bolshevists have
plunged the Russian masses into an abyss of
misery and privation never experienced under the
worst of the Tzars. Francis, Fox and Paine might
sneer at Burke's sentimentalism; but that he spoke
the feelings of Englishmen of every class was
proved at one end of the social scale by the huge
sale of "the book [1] which every gentleman ought
to read", as the King said, and at the other end by
the burning of Dr. Priestley's house at Birmingham, however we may censure the manner in
which the masses testified their loyalty to Church
and Crown.

In April of 1795 Warren Hastings was called
to the Bar of the House of Lords, eight years after
he had been impeached there, solemnly informed
from the Woolsack that he was acquitted, and dis-
charged. A year before in the House of Commons
the managers of the impeachment were thanked,
somewhat coldly. Burke immediately applied for
the Chiltern Hundreds, and retired to Beaconsfield, not without a parting sarcasm at the testi-

---

[1] The *Reflections on the French Revolution* reached fourteen
editions, and 30,000 copies were sold in the first six years,
big figures in those days.

monials and plaudits which then flowed in from India upon the ex-Governor-General. "He knew", he said, "something of the mythology of the Brahmins. He knew that as they worshipped some gods from love, so they worshipped others from fear. He knew that they erected shrines, not only to the benignant deities of light and plenty, but also to the fiends who preside over smallpox and murder. Nor did he at all dispute the claim of Mr. Hastings to be admitted to such a Pantheon." I agree with Macaulay that this is one of the finest replies ever made in Parliament.

Burke knew that there was little chance of peace in his Sabine farm, though it was comfortable enough, and though he had interests and visitors enough to brighten what Gibbon calls "the browner shade of the evening of life". Prior always speaks of the house as Butler's Court, though Burke, after the first few years, when he called it Gregories, invariably dated his letters from Beaconsfield. Miss Shackleton thus described it:

> Lo! there the mansion stands in princely pride;
> The beauteous wings extend on either side;
> Unsocial pomp flies from the cheerful gate,
> Where hospitality delights to wait.

If we pass "princely pride" to a guest who was an Irish lady and a poetess, the house must have been attractive and considerable, for Mrs. Burke sold it in 1812, just before her death, for £38,500 to Mr. Dupré of Wilton Park. It was burned down in 1813 when in the occupation of a schoolmaster. Burke, like Sir Walter Scott at Abbotsford, had to defend himself against a merciless invasion of strangers, who came to see the statesman, next to Pitt the best-known name in Europe; and the house, whatever its capacity—its owner in warding off a self-invited Frenchman, said it had "very little lodging room"—was always full. "Throw yourself into a coach, come down, and make my house your inn" were Burke's favourite words of invitation. Too many took advantage of the formula in its literal sense. As Beaconsfield is only twenty-four miles from London, there was a constant stream of famous and fashionable people who drove down for the day. There came Arthur Young, a great favourite of Burke's, both as farmer and traveller in France, being perhaps the only agriculturist who made farming pay, and who wrote about it like a man of letters. Mr. Birrell laughs at *Thoughts and Details on Scarcity*, which Burke wrote about this time, and says in

effect that it may be literature but it is not
farming. I suspect that Mr. Birrell thinks it is not
farming, of which he knows nothing, because it is
literature, of which he knows everything. When
the rotation of crops and the price of barley had
been exhausted, Young could always entertain his
host with stories of his travels in devastated France.
There also came the polished and sympathetic
Windham, who had sat by the death-bed of
Johnson, and was soon to perform the same
melancholy office for him whom he strove to cheer
with news of the war. There too appeared the
genial and gentle Sir James Mackintosh, repentant
author of *Vindiciae Gallicae*, dulcifying his recanta-
tion of Jacobinism by copious compliments to the
author of *Reflections on the Revolution*. And was there
not too the lively presence of Mrs. Crewe, that
beautiful and adorable woman of whom we know
so little, the toast of every Whig banquet, who
had deserted the excitement of London routs and
the delights of Devonshire House scandal, to come
and listen to Burke? Besides his duties as host,
Burke had the school for the sons of French
refugees at Penn to look after. With the help of a
small grant from Government, he had bought the
house of a deceased friend, and turned it into a

school for the emigrant children of French parents who had perished by the guillotine or the sword. The boys were dressed by Burke's direction in a blue uniform, wearing in their hats a white cockade inscribed *"Vive le Roi"*; those who had lost their fathers had it placed on a bloody label; those who had lost their uncles on a black one. Burke would walk out on most days to visit his little Royalists, often carrying some delicacy from his larder, such as a haunch of venison, for their table, while recommending the Abbé, their master, not to spare the rod, the recipe of the English public schools for turning out great men. He was once interrupted in the middle of an oration denouncing in robustious Anglo-French to a circle of French nobles the crimes of the Jacobins, by the question, "Mais, enfin, Monsieur, quand est-ce que nous retournerons dans la France? " "Jamais", answered Burke in his loud passionate voice. However, the school was broken up in 1820, after the restoration of Louis XVIII, and the chronicler adds that several of the boys from the Penn school rose to respectable positions in their own country. In keeping with the Penn mood, Burke made a friend drink a glass of sherry, and apologised for not giving him brandy by saying that he would never pay for anything manufactured in France.

With these diversions and occupations it might be thought that Burke had found that repose for which he longed. But three foes beset him. They were, first, his creditors, who, now that he had lost the privilege of Parliament, might at any moment create a scandal. His debts were mountainous and ever rising. A man could not, even in the eighteenth century, keep open house in the country and live in fashionable London lodgings for the sessions of Parliament on nothing. And Burke never had any capital or income. Society was very small in those days, and Burke was one of the most prominent figures. His embarrassment, which was now bordering on beggary, was perfectly well known to the King and the Prime Minister. George III might dine upon boiled mutton, dress plainly and keep a dowdy court; but towards the friends of monarchy he was generosity itself, as his offers to North and Pitt prove. In August 1794 Pitt, with infinite tact and delicacy, wrote to Burke a short official letter, intimating the King's pleasure to grant out of the Civil List a pension of £1200 a year to Mrs. Burke for her life, and to propose to Parliament next session a pension of £2500 a year. There was a good deal of negotiation behind the scenes, carried on between the Prime Minister and the Rev. Walker King, Burke's friend; and finally it was settled that the pension of £1200 should be for the two lives of Burke and his wife; while the pension of £2500 was not brought before Parliament, as Pitt was well aware of the malice of the Foxites, but was granted in October 1795 by the King as a charge on some West India $4\frac{1}{2}$ per cent stock. Morley repeats it as a rumour of the time that Burke sold for £27,500 the pension of £2500 to pay his debts, thus leaving for himself and his wife the £1200 a year and Butler's Court.

The second enemy was his health. The malady which killed Burke, namely, gastric ulcers, was probably caused, certainly aggravated, by his pecuniary worries, and the deaths in the same year of his brother and his son, the two Richards to whom he was passionately attached.

The third enemy was one whom neither the King's warrant nor the waters of Bath could appease. We must remember that the Foxite Whigs hated Burke, much as Gladstonian Liberals hated Joseph Chamberlain, as the traitor who had split the party. Making allowance for this, it is impossible to read without astonishment, and difficult to follow without indignation, the kind of opposition offered by Fox and Sheridan to Pitt's Government in the conduct of a war which, wise or foolish, was a life-and-death struggle with France. The grant of the second pension to Burke happened in the same year as Lord Fitzwilliam's recall from Ireland, and was seized on as an opportunity of attacking Burke and Pitt at the same time. Fox and Sheridan were too prudent to attack anybody's pension, as they doubtless hoped that some day their own debts might be paid in a similar fashion. Indeed there was serious talk at Brookes's of getting up a subscription to pay Fox's card debts, which was the better received as most of the "paper" was held by members of the Club. They were, however, afraid of hurting the feelings of their leader. "How do you think Charles will take it?" inquired an anxious Whig of Selwyn. "Immediately, of course", was the answer. But such was the fascination exercised by Fox over the more dissolute members of the aristocracy that he could always get a vote of censure moved in the House of Lords. The Duke of Norfolk was the first to try conclusions with the author of the *Reflections*, whom he accused of having broken up the Whig Party, and instigated a calamitous war. In a sarcastic and humorous letter to William Elliot, Burke had a preliminary canter with "Jockey of Norfolk", whom nobody treated seriously. The second attack was made at the opening of the session of 1796 by the Duke of Bedford and the Earl of Lauderdale. The grounds of objection were that the grant had been made by the Crown instead of by Parliament; that its reception by an advocate of public economy was inconsistent; and that the amount was excessive. The "old parliamentary hand" must have smiled grimly to himself as he read the report. O that mine adversary would make a speech! His enemies had made speeches, and such speeches as must have gladdened the heart of the most skilful and practised controversialist of the age. Although Burke wrote to a friend in these months, "Alas, my dear friend, I am not what I was two years ago. Society is too much for my nerves. I sleep ill at night, and am drowsy and sleep much in the day"; and although one of his guests at Butler's Court described him as lounging languidly over the table at meals, with his shirt-sleeves unbuttoned, trying to listen or to talk, the Duke of Bedford's attack acted as a powerful tonic.

He seized his pen, the friend that never failed him, and sat down in 1796, the last year of his life, to write the *Letter* that Prior justly calls "on the whole the most brilliant exhibition of powers perhaps in the whole range of English prose". The minor combatant in the affray may be briefly disposed of. Lord Lauderdale was not a clever man, but he was not a bad fellow. He had been one of Burke's admirers before the party split, and had paid many generous tributes to the protagonist of economic reform. He appears to have repented of his attack upon the pensions of a dying man. He has come down to us spitted on one of Sheridan's best ironies—"a joke in Lauderdale's mouth is no laughing matter".

Francis, fifth Duke of Bedford, was the grandson of John, the fourth Duke, who negotiated for Bute the Treaty of Paris, 1763, and was pelted in the streets on his return and accused of having been bribed by the French. The peace was certainly inglorious, for it gave back many of our conquests; but there is not the slightest evidence that the Duke was other than an honest if an overbearing man. He was venomously assailed by Junius; and those who wish to appreciate the difference between abuse and invective cannot do better than compare

the *Letters* in which Duke John is anonymously
attacked with the *Letter* which Burke addressed to
his grandson. And this gives me an opportunity of
pausing to point out why the *Letter to a Noble Lord*
is not overrated as one of the most perfect pieces
of composition. When we admire a thing as
classical, we ought to know why we do so. Par-
ticularity is the essence of good prose, as it is of
all poetry worthy of the name. The supreme
merit of the *Letter* is the blending of the particular
with the general, the combination of the concrete
with the abstract. Nothing is so nauseous as a
string of personalities unrelieved by argument,
and not used as illustrations of a conclusion. The
Letters of Junius to Duke John are a compilation of
insults which, even if true, are quite irrelevant to
his negotiation of the Treaty. On the other hand,
nothing is more tedious than a series of general
propositions, unenforced by particular instances.
The beauty of the *Letter* consists in the use of each
stroke against the Duke to point a moral;
conversely, the illustration of a general principle
by the citation of a ducal absurdity; and a general
warning to society under cover of the particular
danger to which the Bedford estates might be
exposed. It is also the happiest example of the

antithetical method, of which Macaulay was so fond, and of which the earliest and most famous specimen is to be found in Demosthenes' *On the Crown*. Indeed, the *Letter* may be said in parts to be a string of antitheses.

Burke, like an old hunter, stalked his prey quietly. He had little difficulty in showing that he had earned his pension before taking his seat in Parliament by his study of the nation's laws and history; and that his services to the public during thirty years, more particularly with regard to India and the retrenchment of established expenses, could not be paid for by any pension. Observe the skill of these two strokes. Fox's India Bill, for placing the Government of India in the hands of Whitehall, had been rejected by the House of Lords at the urgent interposition of the King. Burke had been Paymaster of the Forces, and had refused to touch anything but his salary. One of his predecessors had been Charles Fox's father, and the other Rigby, the right-hand man of the Duke of Bedford's father. Both these paymasters had, in accordance with the laxity of the times, been allowed to amass large fortunes out of the handling of the Army and Navy balances. A large slice of this public robbery had been paid by a fond father in liquidation of the debts of Charles. These were palpable hits.

When Burke got within striking distance, he sprang upon his quarry with a sudden ferocity that must be read to be appreciated. The passage beginning, "The grants to the House of Russell were so enormous as not only to outrage economy but even to stagger credibility. The Duke of Bedford is the leviathan among all the creatures of the crown. He tumbles about his unwieldy bulk, he plays and frolics in the ocean of the royal bounty", is probably familiar to many who know little or nothing more of Burke's writing. It is a stock quotation, but Hazlitt said truly that you can no more give an idea of Burke by a quotation than you can give an idea of a house by a brick. People must read him, not all of him, but, as we are all in a hurry nowadays, let them read this *Letter*, which really is a summary or condensation of his political philosophy.

What can be more impressive, and more modern, than his warning to aristocrats and men of property, who dabble in revolutionary ideas, that they will be the first victims of a revolution? The aristocratic or wealthy young Radical is a type frequent enough in all ages from Alcibiades to Equality Philip. The type was fatal to France in the eighteenth century; it was fashionable in England. There were Citizen Stanhope, Pitt's brother-in-law, and Lord Abingdon, and the Duke of Richmond, at all events before the Duchess of Gordon caught him, and Jockey of Norfolk, and Lord Lauderdale who spoilt a story, and young Lord Holland and the Duke of Bedford. A little dashed perhaps by the decapitation of that sportsman the Duke of Orleans, plenty of our gilded youth continued to prattle about Tom Paine and the rights of man. Burke paid the hostile reproaches with a "friendly admonition" to the Woburn Abbey gang.

The persons who have suffered from the cannibal philosophy of France are so like the Duke of Bedford, that nothing but his grace's probably not speaking quite so good French would enable us to find out any difference. A great many of them had as pompous titles as he, and were of full as illustrious a race; some few of them had fortunes as ample; several of them, without meaning the least disparagement to the Duke of Bedford, were as wise, and as virtuous, and as valiant, and as well educated, and as complete in all the lineaments of men of honour, as he is. . . . But security was their ruin. They are dashed to pieces in the storm, and our shores are covered with the wrecks. If they had been aware that such a thing might happen, such a thing never would have happened.

Quite so; security was their ruin.

Burke is the founder of Conservatism. Burkeism, as an energetic living faith, flourished for thirty years, unchecked by Cobbett's *Annual Register*, undaunted by demagogues of the calibre of Brougham, contemptuous even of the onslaughts of Bentham. Obviously it must have reflected the inner consciousness of England, or it could not have endured. What is Burkeism?

In the eighteenth century, from the reign of Queen Anne to the beginning of the war with America, the Whigs were the Conservatives. It may surprise the modern Tory to learn that the creed of the Tories under Anne was annual Parliaments, no standing Army, and no intervention in European politics, the natural reaction against William III's war policy and the predominance of the Marlboroughs. Up with the Church and the Land, and Down with Dissenters and Fundholders, were powerful slogans. After the accession of the Elector and the flight of Bolingbroke, the Tories were divided into the Hanoverian or Whimsical Tories, who disapproved of Bolingbroke and his Treaty of Utrecht, and

many of whom slid off into Whiggism, and the
Jacobite Tories, some of whom "came out" for the
Stuarts in 1715 and 1745, then melted away as an
irreconcilable remnant, "steeped in port and prejudice", as Gibbon might say, until they rallied
round the King and North during the American
War, and ten years later supported Pitt and Burke
in the war against the French Jacobins. Thus do
events fashion parties, for the Tories who ruled
England under Pitt, Perceval, Liverpool, Canning, Castlereagh, Wellington and Peel were
carved out of the old Whig Party. In 1765, when,
by the intervention of a "common friend", Burke
was introduced to Lord Rockingham, the fratri-
cidal war between the Whig gangs was at its
height. Bute, who called himself a Tory on the
accession of George III, had tried "purity and
prerogative" at the election of 1760, and carried
the Treaty of Paris by the bribery of members of
Parliament. But he was soon hustled off by the
Bloomsbury gang, and told to go back to Scotland
with his brother Mackenzie. The beautiful house
which he had begun to build in Berkeley Square
he was obliged to sell hurriedly to Lord Shelburne,
afterwards created Lord Lansdowne. Grenville
succeeded Bute, but he bored everybody, and

Bedford bullied everybody. The mild Rockingham was then allowed to try his hand for a year, and that was the beginning of Burke's career. The speeches on *American Taxation* and *Conciliation with America* were delivered under the North régime, and were corrected for the Press by the orator. The fact that Burke was at this time being paid £700 a year by the American rebels to state their case in Parliament need not diminish our appreciation of the sweeping eloquence and elevation of tone which envelop the notes of our modern colonial policy.

The Parliament of Great Britain sits at the head of her extensive Empire in two capacities: one as the local legislature of this island, providing for all things at home, immediately, and by no other instrument than the executive power. The other, and I think her nobler capacity, is what I call her imperial character; in which, as from the throne of heaven, she superintends all the several inferior legislatures, and guides and controls them all, without annihilating any.

The Imperial Conference could not be more clearly foreshadowed. The power of taxing in Parliament, which includes tariffs, Burke regarded "as an instrument of empire, and not as a means of supply". His idea of an Empire as distinguished from a single State or Kingdom is "that an Empire is the aggregate of many States under one common head, whether this head be a monarch or a presiding republic". The vulgar idea that trade is the cement of empire is thus nobly rebuked:

My hold of the colonies is in the close affection which grows from common names, from kindred blood, from similar privileges, and equal protection. These are ties which, though light as air, are as strong as links of iron.

Let anyone who is disposed to pooh-pooh these sentiments as rhetoric, remember that they were spoken in 1775, and that it was not until a century later, after an interval of Botany Bayism, that our statesmen were forced to adopt them. They may sound to our ears as platitudes, but how must they have sounded in the ears of the Townshends, the Sackvilles and the King?

When Shelburne's peace of 1783 had closed the American question, Burke turned his attention to the Government of India, and it was while the impeachment of Warren Hastings was in full swing that the French Revolution began to absorb the attention of this omnivorous mind. The first outburst of anarchy in Paris, which intoxicated so many shallow politicians in this country, had an opposite effect on Burke. It had the concentrating result of impending calamity, for all the horrors of the reign of terror, which Burke predicted, he imagined to be about to happen to himself and his countrymen. It caused him to meditate deeply on the science and art of governing men, and to give us that series of writings which to-day are the political bible of all who are on the side of law, religion, property and order. Burke is a classic, and therefore can never be out of date.

In the third *Letter on a Regicide Peace* he writes of the ancient divisions of Whigs and Tories as nearly extinct by the growth of new ones, "which have their roots in the present circumstances of the times", and goes on to speak of those persons

who, in the new distribution of parties, consider the Conservation in England of the antient order of things as necessary to preserve order everywhere else, and who regard the general conservation of order in other countries as reciprocally necessary to preserve the same state of things in these lands.

This is the new, the true Conservative Party, which Burke formed in the last decade of the eighteenth century by drawing after him to join Pitt the best of the Whigs, leaving the remnant under the care of Fox and Sheridan. "The Conservation of the antient order of things" is, and ever must be, the foundation of all Conservative parties in all countries and in all ages. Burke ultimately succeeded in making English statesmen see that the war of the French Jacobins was not a war against Louis XVI, but a war against George III, against the King of Prussia, against the Emperor of Austria, against all thrones, against all religion, against all property, against all law, everywhere.

Burke's conviction of the necessity of a strong second Chamber lent colour and force to his picture of what the House of Lords might become under the domination of the Jacobin faction.

As to the House of Lords, it is not worth mentioning. The Peers ought naturally to be the pillars of the Crown: but when their titles are rendered contemptible, and their property invidious, and a part of their weakness and not of their strength, they will be found so many trembling and degraded individuals, who will seek by evasion to put off the evil day of their ruin.[1]

Burke believed in the hereditary principle because

people will not look forward to posterity who never look backward to their ancestors. Besides, the people of England well know that the idea of inheritance

---

[1] *Regicide Peace*, Letter IV.

furnishes a sure principle of conservation, and a sure principle of transmission, without at all excluding a principle of improvement. It leaves acquisition free, but it secures what it acquires.[1]

It should be noted that Burke never uses the word Tory in enforcing his anti-Jacobin policy. As an old Whig he could not with propriety do so; for to a Whig of the eighteenth century a Tory was not a Jacobin, but a Jacobite, in whose breast there survived a hankering after the Stuarts. Even five or six years later, in 1795, when he was writing the "Regicide Letters", and Pitt and Portland at least were avowed Tories, he never used the word. Burke's favourite word, in opposition to the innovating policies of Fox and Sheridan, who had begun to flirt with Parliamentary Reform, was Conservation.

Burke thought that prejudice, with conscious or unconscious reason behind it, was a good thing, because it is of ready application in an emergency, and renders a man's virtue his habit. He was afraid to put men to live and trade each on his own private stock of reason, because this stock in each man is small, and individuals will do better to avail themselves of the general bank and capital

[1] *Reflections*, p.39.

of nations and of ages. Burke's idea of the State was not that of a universal almoner, but of an intangible corporation or partnership. Tom Paine and the rights of man he answers by saying that men have a right to all the advantages of the society in which they live; to justice; to the fruits of their industry, and to the means of making their industry fruitful.

In this partnership all men have equal rights, but not to equal things. He that has but five shillings in the partnership has as good a right to it as he that has five hundred pounds has to his larger proportion. But he has not a right to an equal dividend in the product of the joint stock.

This is a truth that is steadily ignored to-day, because the five-shillingers have so many more votes than the five-hundreders.

The plunder of the rich was going on across the Channel, and Burke impressed on his countrymen its injustice and folly:

Monied men ought to be allowed to set a value on their money; if they did not, there could be no monied men. This desire of accumulation is a principle without which the means of their service to the State could not exist. The love of lucre, though sometimes carried to a ridiculous, sometimes to a vicious excess, is the grand cause of prosperity to all States.

Nothing excited Burke's scorn more vividly than the cant, as prevalent then as now, about the sufferings of the working classes:

We have heard many plans for the relief of the "Labouring Poor". This puling jargon is not as innocent as it is foolish. In meddling with great affairs, weakness is never innoxious. Hitherto the name of Poor (in the sense in which it is used to excite compassion) has not been used for those who can, but for those who cannot labour—for the sick and infirm; for orphan infancy, for languishing and decrepid age; but when we affect to pity as poor those who must labour or the world can not exist, we are trifling with the condition of mankind.

As I have shown above, Burke was in his own neighbourhood the most open-handed and charitable of men, with nothing of pedantry in his giving. Once walking with a lady in a country lane they were accosted by a tramp to whom Burke gave money. His companion scolded him, and asked how he could give money which he knew would go in gin. "Madam," said Burke, "the man is old; gin is his pleasure: therefore let him have gin." In his *Thoughts on Scarcity*, he told the poor that they were only poor because they were numerous, and he detested the "mumping cant" of a hunger-bitten philanthropy which insulted their intelligence without relieving their demands.

This affected pity only tends to dissatisfy them with their condition, and to teach them to seek resources where no resources are to be found—in something else than their own industry, and frugality, and sobriety.

What with America, India, Ireland and the French Revolution, Burke had little time for that branch of politics which looms so large to-day, economic legislation, and the interference of the State in the business affairs of its citizens. The amateur farmer has long been a standing butt for raillery, and Burke's earnestness about runts and roots diverted attention from the solid value of his *Thoughts and Details on Scarcity*. He was, as might be expected, a stern opponent of the zealots of the sect of regulation, especially with regard to the people's food, and the proposals which crop up periodically that the Government should buy corn. It is a perilous thing to try experiments on the farmer, as his capital is far more feeble than commonly is imagined. "The moment that Government appears at market all the principles of market will be subverted" is a truth which Socialists would do well to ponder, especially as some of them are considering bulk purchases of food by the Government from the Dominions. The matter is summed up in the conclusion that the State ought to confine itself to what regards the State, or the creatures of the State, namely, the exterior establishment of its religion, its magistracy, its revenue, its military force by sea and land; the corporations that owe their existence to its fiat; in a word, to everything that is truly and properly public, to the public peace, to the public safety, to the public order, to the public prosperity.

Statesmen who know themselves will, with the dignity which belongs to wisdom, proceed only in this the superior orb and first mover of their duty. . . . But as they descend from the State to a province, and from a province to a parish, and from a parish to a private house, they go on accelerated in their fall. They cannot do the lower duty, and in proportion as they try it they will certainly fail in the higher. They ought to know the different departments of things; what belongs to laws, and what manners alone can regulate. To these great politicians may give a leaning, but they can not give a law.

To modern statesmen all this will be flat blasphemy.

Much of Burke's writing against the French

Revolution is properly devoted to "telling off" the actors in that tragedy, and might with only a change of names be addressed to the Bolsheviks, who so improved upon their model that they have murdered and robbed a million and a half where Robespierre and Co. murdered and robbed thousands. But it does not, except incidentally, contain the essence of his Toryism, which is reserved for the *Letter* which follows. Burke seemed to gather up his arguments and fling them with all his might at the Duke of Bedford in that impressive and majestic warning that we are all of us safe only so long as the Sovereign and the Constitution are safe. The passage is so famous as to be hackneyed and trite. But were it worn to tatters I would quote it again:

As long as the well-compacted structure of our Church and State, the sanctuary, the holy of holies of that ancient law, defended by reverence, defended by power, a fortress at once and a temple, shall stand inviolate on the brow of the British Sion—as long as the British monarchy, not more limited than fenced by the orders of the State, shall, like the proud keep of Windsor, rising in the majesty of proportion, and girt with the double belt of its kindred and coeval towers, as long as this awful structure shall oversee and guard the subjected land—so long the mounds and dykes of the low, fat, Bedford level will have nothing to fear from all the pickaxes of all the levellers of France. As long as our Sovereign Lord the King, and his faithful subjects, the lords and commons of this realm, the triple cord, which no man can break; the solemn, sworn, constitutional frank-pledge of the nation, the firm guarantees of each other's being and each other's rights; the joint and several securities, each in its place and order, for every kind and every quality, of property and of dignity;—so long as these endure, so long the Duke of Bedford is safe; and we are all safe together—the high from the blights of envy and the spoliations of rapacity; the low from the iron hand of oppression and the insolent spurn of contempt.

Burke's Toryism, revolved in his mind for years, was evoked and crystallised by the massacres and confiscations of the French Revolution. He wrote down the horror and fear which he felt in words which burnt themselves into the conscience of his contemporaries. His writings, besides containing imperishable truths about the science and art of government, were a living testament on which the Tory Party thrived for thirty years. The majority of Englishmen, in the first two decades of the nineteenth century, were really afraid of a subversion of society by Jacobin agitators, as they called Parliamentary reformers. But by the third decade Burke's Toryism began to wear thin. The fear of the Revolution grew fainter, and the industrial distress, caused by the war and the introduction of machinery, was very near and very real. Burkeism was banished for the time by the Reform Act of 1832, which, as has often been pointed out, was a disfranchising more than an enfranchising measure. It destroyed the pocket boroughs and the corporation boroughs, the first serious blow at the power of the peerage, and enthroned the £10 householder of the middle class. It was not in the least a democratic measure, and the agitation which preceded it subsided, not because more people voted, but because trade revived.

THE END